RADIO CONGO

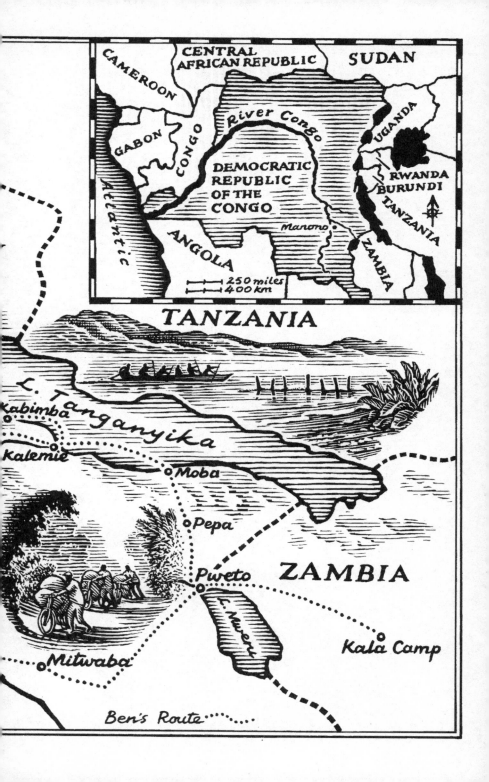

RADIO CONGO

Signals of Hope from
Africa's Deadliest War

BEN RAWLENCE

ONEWORLD

A Oneworld Book

First published by Oneworld Publications 2012

Copyright © Ben Rawlence 2012

The moral right of Ben Rawlence to be identified as the Author of this
work has been asserted by him in accordance with the Copyright, Designs
and Patents Act 1988

ISBN 978-1-85168-927-9
Ebook ISBN 978-1-78074-095-9

Typeset by Cenveo Publisher Services
Cover design by Dan Mogford
The illustration credits on pp. 291–2 constitute an extension
of this copyright page
Map and ornament artwork copyright © Bill Sanderson 2012
Printed and bound by Bell & Bain, UK

Oneworld Publications
185 Banbury Road Oxford, OX2 7AR, England

Stay up to date with the latest books,
special offers, and exclusive content from
Oneworld with our monthly newsletter

Sign up on our website
www.oneworld-publications.com

MIX
Paper from
responsible sources
FSC® C007785

Still there are too many people in Europe who only know how Africans are dying, not how they live.

HENNING MANKELL

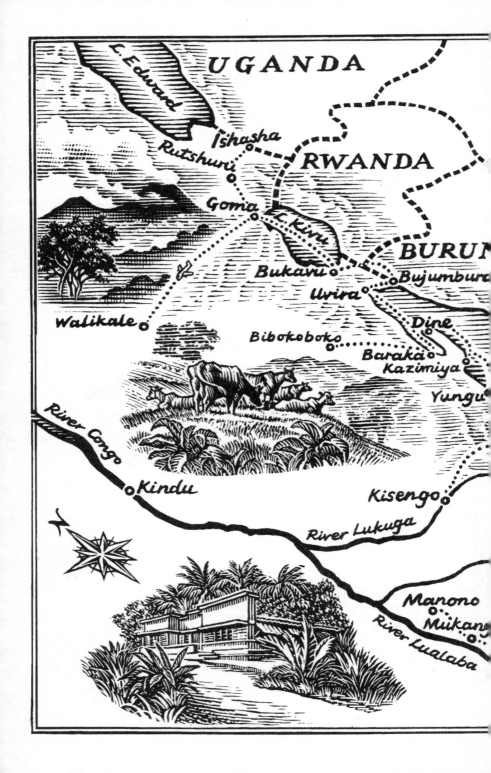

Contents

Prologue

IN MANONO, THE RADIO sits on a small four-legged wooden stool in the mud, its aerial bent in several places, the battery door held together with tape. Arranged in a rough circle around it are about twenty men and several women, sitting on benches, chairs and upturned crates; a few are leaning against the pine trees that rustle quietly in the night breeze. They are priests, nuns, teachers, a waitress. Some hold their chins in their hands, others pull on cigarettes, and every now and then an exclamation goes up in reaction to the news. The radio speaks of war in the north, of politics in Kinshasa and of more war in Iraq. An orange moon lies sullen in the treetops that frame the compound where we sit, but I am the only one admiring it.

Manono lies deep in the forest on the upper reaches of the Congo River in the east of the country, four days' ride on a motorbike from the shores of Lake Tanganyika. The main road linking it to the other towns of the east has been destroyed; goods arrive by barge or on the occasional humanitarian organisation plane that, when the weather allows, lands on the old airstrip. The people listening to the radio know what is happening in Baghdad but have little idea about the news from the town of Kongolo, several days' journey up the river, or Mitwaba, five days' walk to the south. Like thousands of other towns emerging from Congo's recent wars, Manono is an island in a sea of forest. News reaches Manono but news of Manono rarely reaches anywhere.

RADIO CONGO

1

The lost city

Manono, 1966

A WIDE GRAVEL DRIVE leads up to a house. A car stands in front. The house is rectangular and so is the covered veranda that looks out over a lush tropical garden. The shadows of tall trees creep across the drive and obscure half of the house. The visible half is a fiesta of right angles: a jutting roof above the porch, square windows and sharp flat slabs that cap a wide ridge of concrete on the upper floor. From the way the light bounces off the shiny surface of the car, it seems to be the middle of a hot afternoon. Perhaps the master and mistress are having a siesta and barefoot, uniformed servants are sweeping the floors. Is there a figure in the doorway; is that a slight lightening of the shadow, a white face peeking out at the jungle?

Opposite the house in the old photograph, beyond its frame, are other villas of modern design. One is smaller, with a stepped roof in imitation of a medieval castle, and geometric patterns scored in the concrete walls. A veranda slices the house in two, like a knife through fruit. The windows of the one next door are round portholes, painted blue, two on the front and one on the side, giving the house the look of a ship beached among the palms. Beyond is another fanciful villa, with a long curving façade, next to that another, then another, the houses dotted through a forest that has been fenced and thinned into garden but which nevertheless threatens to swallow, at a moment's notice, this beautiful art deco suburb.

The street is made of marram; crushed and pressed gravel. It bears the fresh tyre marks of elegant automobiles: Citroens, Renaults, and Peugeots, with long running boards, rounded bonnets and polished hubcaps. At the end of the street is a pair of huge mango trees, which shade one end of a swimming pool that otherwise shimmers in the heat. Black and white children splash, or hurl themselves off the high board under the careful gaze of lifeguards. From his little wooden hut, the attendant comes out to sweep the paving stones and collect any mangoes that fall into the pool during the season.

Bordering the pool is the school; its oblong walls cut with tall metal windows arranged in neat symmetrical lines. Beyond, tennis courts lie hot and red, their brushed clay smooth and calm against the unruly thatch of the elephant grass. Behind the courts lies the golf course; rich, green, billiard-table baize, pocked with sand, where men in white circle, halt, swing and pirouette like dancers in a strange, slow-motion ballet.

The road curves past the golf course and the tennis courts in a wide arc strung with electricity pylons, until it reaches a small roadblock. There, policemen salute and raise the barrier for the cars of those who live in the wealthy quarter so they may drive down the long, broad avenue towards the cathedral, with black tiles and a gabled roof; a Flemish refugee adrift in the African bush.

The streets of the town are lined with little box hedges that squat beneath telegraph poles. In the centre is a huge four-storey brewery that makes beer for export across the region. At the end of another wide boulevard, fringed with mango trees, looms the mine works: the source of the town's prosperity and the region's wealth. It is a massive operation, employing thirty thousand people and state-of-the-art technology: Africa's only tin works, smelting its own ores and exporting pure metal. The tailings form a great towering white mountain that matches in its tidy geometry the modernist cubes of the villas in the town below.

This is the town of Manono in the newly independent, former Belgian colony of Congo. The airport terminal has an arched doorway, and a rectangular tower that looks as if it were made of Lego. Here, other Belgian, French, British, German, Greek, Portuguese, South African and Lebanese colonists from across central Africa touch down for a holiday, a tantalizing taste of 'modern' civilisation away from their jobs but closer to home than Europe, weeks away by boat. New planes are beginning to hop across the continents but they still take a while.

The Belgian mining company Géomines has made Manono into a model modern town. Wealthy visitors stroll down the boulevards, lamp-lit courtesy of the hydroelectric power station. The *supermarché*, in its sleek whitewashed skin, over three storeys high, is stocked with all the latest European products, as well as beer, meat and dairy goods from Katanga's modern farms and factories. Well-dressed white teenagers in the cafés near the petrol station perch on red leather, listen to rock-and-roll, and eat ice creams, just like their peers in the USA.

Nineteen-sixties Manono a Corbusier dream lit by Edward Hopper, a modernist experiment in the jungle.

This was the city I glimpsed in 2007, in old promotional photos of Manono and Katanga province, published by Belgian mining companies in the 1950s and 60s in the dog days of Belgian rule and on the cusp of independence, to reassure investors, and perhaps themselves, that things wouldn't change with the end of European rule. The sharply focused prints on the glossy pages of the thick brown volume were so at odds with what we hear of Congo now – war, rape and conflict minerals – that it seems almost impossible that at one point this city built on tin was wealthier and more advanced than some European towns wracked by post-war deprivation. The Belgian modernist architects of Manono, working in the 40s and 50s, thought that they were building a scientific future full of optimism, progress and hope. Seeing that dreamy hopeful vision expressed in concrete, I wondered what had become of those ideals, of Manono, of Congo?

I came across the photos in the library of my Alma Mater, the School of Oriental and African Studies in London, as I was planning a trip to eastern Congo and Lake Tanganyika in 2007. Elections had passed relatively calmly the previous October and peace seemed to be settling, despite some flare-ups around the city of Goma, in the province of North Kivu. I wanted to visit the country as it emerged from conflict, to share in Congo's post-war experience and see where the future might lead – to peace or back to war.

In the map room, I requested all the maps of eastern Congo they had. The librarian brought out the original Royal Geographical Society maps of Lake Tanaganyika, drawn by Speke and Burton in 1858; they were stored in a scuffed red paper folder with a drawstring. Then came the Belgian colonial maps, 70s atlases of Zaire, and some military flying charts, dominated by huge white spaces where no surveys had been done.

Eventually, I found Manono, on a bend of one of the main tributaries of the Congo River, in northern Katanga province. It was on its own, far from any other towns, with a little symbol for an airstrip. Several roads led to it but I suspected those to be of little use nowadays. It was hundreds of miles south of the conflict zone in the north and hundreds more miles from the capital of Katanga province, Lubumbashi, on the Zambian border. Lake Tanganyika was far to the east. Manono's only connection to this vast nation, this vast continent, seemed to be the river curving away west to the Atlantic.

I began to ask how I might get there. The more I researched, the less I knew. I tried to find out about the logistics of travelling south along Lake Tanganyika, about the security situation and the likelihood of finding a boat. No one had any idea. The United Nations had a few patchy reports, the most useful information being that the roads on the maps no longer existed. No foreign journalist had filed from outside the main towns in the conflict zones farther north in recent years. A leading Congo analyst, who had followed the war for years, told me: 'Sorry mate, never been south of Uvira'.

Yet south of Uvira is a vast territory that until very recently had been ravaged by war. Lake Tanganyika is over six hundred miles long and borders the provinces of South Kivu and Katanga, a region larger than France, half a million square kilometres, a huge area of a huge country where the conflict was beginning to recede. I thought that there, in this big silent quarter, must be hundreds of stories waiting to be told. If I could reach Manono, I could find out how the people had fared during the war and catch a glimpse of what peace might look like.

Unlike the foreign correspondents who dash in and out of towns that they can reach by plane when the fighting flares up, I resolved to travel slowly, overland, starting with the warring north-east and moving down the lake through the silent south-eastern quarter of the country, that huge chunk between Lake Tanganyika and the Congo River. And finally, although I had no idea how, I would arrive at the modernist dream on the river under its square mountain of tin: Manono.

2

'What you wanna go there for?'

A traditional wooden canoe on the Burundi shore of Lake Tanganyika

'CONGO, NOW WHAT YOU wanna go there for?' asks
Jim in a drawling, slightly drunken, southern American
accent. Jim is a big man. One of the biggest I've seen. He
used to be in the US Special Forces and says he has fought
in every major world conflict since Vietnam, even those in
which the US was not involved.

'Because the United States is never not involved.'

Jim and a dozen other mercenaries are sitting around
a low cane table by the hotel pool, enticingly aglow with
underwater lamps. If you only saw the men's feet, in matching white socks and sandals, you might think this a meeting
of missionaries. They are here in Bujumbura under con-
tract from the US government, to train the Burundian
military. At least that's what they tell me.

The hotel looks out over Lake Tanganyika; the hills
on the opposite shore are Congolese. The silent quarter to
which I'm heading extends west through those hills, to
Manono and the Congo River and thousands of miles
beyond. I have come here *en route* to the conflict zone
around Goma, to assess the security situation across the
lake. Apparently, there have been clashes recently but no
one in Burundi seems to know a thing. After several days
knocking around Bujumbura, I haven't found anyone who's
been in Congo, apart from these guys, but the mercenaries
are cagey.

'Of course, I ain't never been to the Congo officially
but I can tell you, you don't wanna be goin' there', Jim
warns.

Even after an armful of beers, these guys don't let
their guard drop. Jim is proud his son has followed in his
footsteps by joining the Special Forces but prays that he
won't be sent to Iraq. Ricky, a weathered ex-soldier from
Tennessee, shortened his jail term by joining the French

Foreign Legion, although he almost regretted his decision when his initiation involved crawling through a cage of baboons with a rucksack stuffed full of bananas. Frank, the quiet one, with narrow spectacles, specializes in 'technology'. Their world is a scary place, where nothing is certain, life is cheap, and life's pleasures should be enjoyed when they present themselves.

These are exactly the kind of people I don't want to meet. They are generous and funny and revealing about their lives, but not about the lives of those I want to talk to – the Congolese. Instead, I am drunk with Americans. There are reasons for that, of course. As Jim says, the US is always involved somehow. Many different histories have brought us to this place, at this moment, all of them involving Congo's unfortunate geology. Blessed with deposits of ninety per cent of the world's minerals, Congo will forever be a place where foreign soldiers have to pretend they haven't been.

A lot is at stake in those dark hills, whose crisp perforated ridge is just visible against the darkening sky and beyond the glow of the pool: gold, tin, coltan, wolframite, manganese, copper and diamonds. The mercenaries know better than me but they don't ask too many questions about my trip. Instead, they give me a gallon of water and advise me not to trust anyone at all. When I try to disagree, they just smile, equating my innocence either with being European or lacking combat experience, or both.

'Tell us, Ben, how does it feel to be British?' asks Ricky, to roars of laughter.

Despite being fascinated as a boy with the river and the jungle, the stories of Livingstone meeting alien African societies for the first time, and of course Tarzan and Tintin, I had never really considered going to Congo. For all my adult life, the country had been at war. When I left school I went to Africa, to Tanzania, to spend nine months attempting to teach English to very patient and generous students in a quiet, pretty school on the slopes of Mount Kilimanjaro. I first became properly aware of Zaire, as it then was, one morning in April 1994, when the maths teacher with whom I shared a house came running into the living room wrapped in a towel, shaking his large Chinese radio with both hands.

'Listen, listen, the rivers are running red!'

The Rwandan genocide had begun. Long-standing rivalries and political tensions were distilled into a flammable mist of hate that issued from the extremist Hutu radio stations, first among them the infamous *Radio Télévision Libre des Mille Collines*. A tide of Rwandan Tutsi refugees flooded into Tanzania and the rivers that flowed down from the hills of Rwanda into Lake Victoria did indeed turn a shocking red. The Hutu *genocidaires*, the perpetrators, fled the other way, into Zaire, along with two million Hutu refugees, almost a third of Rwanda's population.

I didn't know it then but the genocide in Rwanda was to lead directly to the unravelling of Zaire and its rebirth as the war-wracked Democratic Republic of Congo. The slaughter of Tutsis and the mass exodus of Hutus into Congo acted as a catalyst, turning the low-level tension and violence between different Congolese ethnic groups and political factions into what has been called Africa's first 'World War'. It was a war that was to last for over a decade, drawing in a dozen foreign countries, making refugees of tens of millions and leaving over four million dead – four times the death toll of the genocide.

Two years later, in 1996, I was back in Tanzania, learning Swahili at the University of Dar-es-Salaam. With my fellow students, I listened in wonder to the news on the radio of the unlikely success of the rebels marching on Kinshasa in wellington boots. In September, Rwanda invaded Zaire, in hot pursuit of Hutu militias who were rearming in the refugee camps around Goma. But after they had hunted and massacred as many Hutus as they could find, including bombing refugee camps and slaughtering women and children, they didn't return home. Around half a million refugees were pushed back into Rwanda, while the former Hutu government, army and *Interahamwe* militia, along with another half a million people, fled further west, deeper into Zaire.

Rwanda decided that the leopard-skin-wearing dictator of Zaire, Mobutu Sese Seko, could not be trusted to eliminate the Hutu threat that threatened to fester in his nation's vast eastern forests. Other regional powers had also tired of Mobutu and plotted his removal. Now was their moment. With foreign help, and the blessing of the United States, Rwanda's new Tutsi government confected what looked like an indigenous Congolese rebel movement made up of ethnic Tutsis, which the Rwandan army propelled across the country, almost unopposed, to end Mobutu's thirty-two-year reign in 1997. The puppet rebel leader who succeeded Mobutu as president and renamed Zaire as the Democratic Republic of Congo, was called Laurent Désiré Kabila.

For a few fragile years, Kabila struggled to get to grips with the wreckage that Mobutu had left behind: an empty treasury, a mining industry that had become the dictator's personal bank account, a bureaucracy choked with nepotism, a country whose infrastructure was a memory. Kabila tried to assert himself and emerge from Rwanda's shadow but when he ordered the Rwandan forces to go home, they turned on him.

This second war proved to be much bloodier than the first, as shifting alliances between Congo's neighbours and the promise of mineral loot caused Uganda, Angola, Zimbabwe, Namibia, Sudan, Chad and Libya to intervene on different sides. The writer Gérard Prunier likened the Congolese war to the Thirty Years' War in the seventeenth century, in which Poland was simply the battleground for plunder and the settling of scores among European elites, and nothing to do with the interests of the people who lived on the land.

Most foreign countries withdrew from Congo following the 'all-inclusive peace agreement', signed in South Africa in December 2002, but the Congolese government did not control the whole country. The number of players had been reduced but the game was not over. The war died down but refused to die out completely as the Congolese national army contended with Mai Mai militias run by local warlords who were out of control, and with invading Rwandan and Ugandan forces who were making too much money out of mining to want to go home.

Laurent Kabila was assassinated in 2001; his son Joseph, just twenty-nine years old, claimed the presidency. When the transitional government set up by the all-inclusive agreement finally delivered real elections in 2006, Joseph became the first democratically elected leader of Congo since Patrice Lumumba, who had been assassinated in 1961. Holding elections in a country still at war might seem like a foolish idea, and the polls were indeed followed by violence. In the capital, Kinshasa, forces loyal to opposition leader Jean-Pierre Bemba went on the rampage; in the Kivus, Laurent Nkunda, a rebel general who had fought for Rwanda during the war (and who still took his orders from Kigali), went on the offensive.

By 2007 Bemba was in exile, the subject of an arrest warrant from the International Criminal Court. Conflict had subsided in most of Congo, although Nkunda was still fighting in North Kivu, the eastern province in which the war had started a decade earlier. I began, after ten years working in different parts of Africa, to think about a visit. Congo remained the most fascinating, beguiling and, I suspected, misunderstood country on the continent and I wanted to see it for myself.

With the mercenaries' admonitions ringing in my ears, I sit on the shore of Lake Tanganyika, staring at the hills of eastern Congo twenty miles away. The mountains look inscrutable; they bring sunset an hour early to Bujumbura, so high into the sky do they reach. The rain that falls on those hills drains into the Lualaba, the Lukuga and the many tributaries that form the mighty Congo River, which cuts across the plains, past Manono and the countless other towns in the interior, away to the west, to the sea.

My stopover in Burundi has yielded precisely nothing about the logistics of going south down the lake and provided zero reassurance about my hunch that an absence of news reports from the remote and seldom-visited areas far away from Goma means an absence of fighting. But who knows? If a gun goes off in a forest and no one hears it, did it really fire? I guess there's nothing for it but to leap and hope, trust the people who live there to feed me, give me shelter and help me along to the next place, contrary to everything the mercenaries say. I shall have to see whether the famous Swahili hospitality has survived the war intact.

The night draws down like a blind; the mountains form a black wall against the fading pinks of the sky. At the foot of the hills, one by one, sprinkles of yellow lights appear. There are people there, somewhere, cooking dinner, putting children to bed, settling in for the night.

3

Under the volcano

Volcanic debris in the streets of Goma

THE APPROACH TO GOMA airport is over Lake Kivu, so that planes coming in to land skim low over the water and aim straight for the volcano that stands sentinel behind the town. As we perform this manoeuvre, the co-pilot opens the window to decrease cabin pressure, a strange procedure that makes me grip my seat a little more tightly. He then leans out with a video camera to record the approach over the lake. My knuckles whiten. Is this normal? The dashboard labels are handwritten and the passenger cabin is choked with the fumes of aviation fuel. When we're safely down, I joke with the pilot about the ropey plane.

'Are you kidding?' he replies in all seriousness. 'This is the only plane in Goma with an international aviation licence.'

The war started here. The waves of violence that flowed westwards through Congo had their origin in the sinewy history of the Kivu provinces in the far east. Rwanda is just up the hill from the runway. Kigali is fewer than two hundred kilometres away. Like a volcano that has spread its lava across the land but is still smouldering and may yet have another bellyful of fire to share, North Kivu is the caldera and Goma its capital.

I begin to ask around among the journalists and UN staff for anyone with news of Manono and that is how, one night over a tableful of expensive beers, I meet a man shaped like a barrel and with a laugh like a hyena: the journalist and impresario Jean-Baptiste. J-B runs a radio station called Racou FM in Rutshuru, the front line in the conflict zone, just outside Goma but he occasionally travels to Manono to help Radio Manono, the station there. He thinks my plan to travel overland to Manono is the funniest thing since the Congolese government tried to send a rocket – no more than a firework really – into space.

'But there is a plane, an airport, you can fly from here!' he shouts, pressing his sides and slapping a hand on the table. I try to explain the value of travelling slowly, talking to people, understanding the war and its effects.

'Ahh, you're a journalist. Like me', he says, and the smile leaves his face, as though being a journalist were a mournful thing.

'Radio is the spider's web that is holding this country together', he proclaims grandly.

He explains that, in this devastated land, local radio stations are a community's ears, the receivers of news from the rest of the world for people cut off by lack of roads, impossible terrain or the price of petrol and phone calls. And they are its eyes; the beacons of warning or hope that transmit the goings-on in a town to the surrounding countryside, creating and defining an association among those who live within its range. Those who work in radio are the best informed, he says, and he urges me to seek out the radio stations and local journalists to help me as I venture into the more remote parts of the east.

'But first, you must see Goma', he insists.

Goma's hotels are a revolving hot desk for war reporters, most of whom file from here. I had therefore planned to avoid the town but, as J-B points out to me with his wagging finger and cackling laugh, to do so would be like trying to understand the south of England without visiting London or to understand Cuba without seeing Havana. Goma is a carnival of war, money and minerals; the heart of the conflict economy that pumps real blood around the east.

'To truly understand the war', J-B proclaims, 'you need to follow the cash'. And he hands me the number of a tax collector, Olivier.

Mount Nyiragongo, an active volcano, towers over Goma town. At night the sky above the crater simmers orange and passing clouds catch a spark and burn red. When the national park is not over-run by rebels and when the volcano is not threatening to erupt, it is possible to climb the mountain and camp on its rim, looking down at the boiling rock a thousand feet below.

Life here is precarious, under threat from sky, land and lake, which is full of dissolved methane that has seeped from underwater fissures. Goma is on a geological fault line as well as a political one and this lends the place an edge, an urgency. When I visit, the town is full of rumours about a forthcoming strike against the rebel general, Laurent Nkunda, who, though he fought under the elder Kabila in 1996, has accused his son of corruption and has defied the Congolese army since 2004. The people fear that, if provoked, Nkunda will simply take Goma. It's no wonder that its inhabitants aren't living for tomorrow, they are living for today.

What that means of course depends on who you are. Some are living day to day, while others are spending money like there's no tomorrow. You have to be almost schizophrenic to survive in Goma. For the refugees who pour out of the countryside in waves and wash up on the shores of Lake Kivu, life is miserable, and it is their stories – of rape, violence, helplessness – that most frequently adorn foreign newspapers. 'Rape Epidemic Raises Trauma of War' and 'Congo on the Edge of War' reports the *New York Times* during my visit to the east. For thousands, life caught between Nkunda and the Congolese army is horrific but for others, war is good for business. The shocking, untold story of Goma is that it is a boom town; the fates of the refugees and the businessmen are bound together. This is what J-B wants me to see and for the next few days he sets out to show me the money trail.

Olivier is an imposing six foot three, with large hands and broad shoulders. He shows up to meet me in a brown and white pin-stripe suit, with oiled hair and pointy brown shoes. His face has been bleached so that it is a shade or two lighter than his hands but not yet the burnt red of the more ambitious bleaching operations favoured by Congolese women. He proves to be the perfect guide. As we stroll around the market he grants nearly everyone a nod, a smile or, for a chosen few, a handshake.

As far as I can understand, the tax system in Goma works as a kind of franchise. Olivier collects a percentage from all the traders, usually negotiable, depending on how well they are doing or how badly he needs the money. He then pays dues to the municipality and stops the local government from preying on the traders. He isn't armed but the arrangement has the feel of a protection racket. He says there is a lot of competition and that it's very hard work, although on today's evidence it is difficult to see where the work part might come in.

Olivier walks me through the closely knit neighbourhood of Goma's commercial district. The streets are a constant mess of puddles and lava – a souvenir of the most recent eruption, in 2002, when Nyiragongo blanketed the town with a sheet of molten rock. Lava flowed straight

down the main high street, streaming into shops and setting them on fire. The residents, resourceful as ever, simply
graded the rock, made it into a road and moved the shops
up a floor.

Behind the high street and between the concrete
buildings are tiny wooden shacks with tin roofs, from which
an incessant clatter of sewing machines rings out. Brightly-
coloured cloth of every possible pattern festoons their
outsides. Busy tailors are a sign of prosperity; new clothes
are not cheap.

Nor are cars. In Goma, traffic jams are an everyday
occurrence; the narrow roads are not wide enough for all
the motorbikes, trucks, black-windowed four-wheel drives
and pedestrians that jostle atop the lava. A motorbike
totters by, with a twenty-foot-long bowed pole mounted on
the back, from which dangle hundreds of loaves of bread.
Female porters carry enormous loads on their heads, sweat
pouring down their puffing faces. Children sit on oil drums
by the roadside, selling dirty red fuel in Coke bottles, and
through every crowd thread young men trailing lianas of
scratch cards for mobile phones. The town courses with
energy, as though the volcano is breathing down everyone's
neck.

This is the daily reality for the inhabitants of the war-
ravaged east: a permanent state of insecurity that shortens
horizons and intensifies the now. Plans beyond a few days
ahead in such circumstances are considered foolish and no
one can say with any certainty what I might find around the
next corner, let alone hundreds of miles south on the road
to Manono.

The next day, just as the sky is turning purple, making
the volcano loom larger than ever in the dusk, I get a phone
call. It's J-B.

'We're going dancing. Come to the stadium, now', he says.

I find J-B in an Internet café built into the side of the *stade de l'unité*, along with three other journalist colleagues, all desperately filing their stories by the light of a single dirty bulb. We must queue to cross the road on a set of stepping stones that span the giant puddles. When we get to the other side J-B knocks on the door of what looks like a cupboard. Two narrow shutters open to reveal a shop selling a mix of candles, batteries, sweets and nylon under-wear; the usual. Two men are counting large amounts of dollars on the top of a wooden box.

'My wife's family', announces J-B.

The men look up and nod while their fingers con-tinue fluttering among the notes, unconcerned. We leave our bags there for safekeeping and cross the stepping stones back to Nova, J-B's favourite bar. It is only seven o'clock on a Friday night but the place is jumping with people. They are dancing to music: *bolingo*.

Bolingo, sometimes called *ndombolo*, is derived from soukous, Congo's signature guitar-driven music that sprang from the ubiquitous 'rumba' of the 30s and 40s. It's a six-eight shuffle, speeded up, strung together with fast, high and ever-so-sweet melodic guitar and accompanied by what can only be described as crooning. 'Bolingo' means 'I love you' in Lingala, the Bantu language widely spoken in Congo, and is the subject of so many of the songs that the term came to denote the music itself.

The song blaring through Nova changes, and an entire table of well-dressed, middle-aged people leap to their feet, sending drinks and chairs flying. On the dance floor men in suits and women in fine fabrics grab each other and grind manically.

A succession of suitors comes to chat to J-B. Pierre, a lawyer with gold cufflinks and a huge Rolex, says Goma's frantic air is caused by money. He complains that the booming economy has accelerated the decline of the judicial system. It has become, he says, 'a catastrophe'. Previously, the judges wanted one hundred dollars for a decision; now they want five hundred dollars, even a thousand. The more they eat the more they want.

'The war here is about money, too. Tribalism is not the main problem in Congo – it is money of any colour', he says.

Two government men in smart trousers and regulation pointy shoes and gold watches stay longer than the rest. They are wearing 'Save the Gorilla' t-shirts: NGO chic. J-B is wearing one stamped MONUC – the ultimate status symbol in Goma, the brand of the UN peacekeepers.

I ask one of the government men about taxes and why Congo doesn't do more to curb the smuggling of tin, gold and timber over the border into Rwanda, a trade that loses the national treasury millions of dollars a year and fuels the continuing conflict. He can't see the problem. Goma is thriving, people are working, life is good. A beringed finger waves at the people dancing violently and with hot boozy breath he croaks 'do these people think there is a war on?'

It's getting dark when I leave. I retrieve my bag and walk down the road, searching for a taxi or a moped. I must look a little forlorn standing in the shadows of the tall dark trees, because a car's headlights pick me out and a battered Toyota comes into view and crunches to a halt. Three young men

peer out and offer me a lift. They are freelance tax collec-
tors, like Olivier, collecting levies on coltan, tin, petrol and
shops. They think I am a businessman. A white man not
working for a charity in Goma must be after money, they
say, as if there is no other reason to be here.

'A tourist? No. That's not possible. You are researching business, mining, aviation, what is it?'

I try to assure them otherwise but they are unconvinced. They are full of optimism at the money to be made
in Goma, if only one had some capital and they cannot
believe that I don't want to go into business with them.

'That's a shame. If you want to do petrol business
here we could really talk, *vraiment*! Think about it, it's a
great business', says one.

They propose that I would import the petrol from
Rwanda or Uganda and they would take care of all the
paperwork. Their terms are vague: 'There would be
some that goes to the government, and then there is our
discussion…'

The biggest opportunities, according to them, are in
petrol and tin, and tin is the best bet by far. Tin is a large
part of what keeps Goma afloat, and a whole division of the
army busy in mining it. Nearly all that tin comes from one
mine in North Kivu, Bisiye.

Bisiye has long since taken from Manono the mantle of
Congo's largest tin mine. But whereas Manono was a wonder
of mechanisation and heavy industry, a model of twentieth-
century technical know-how, its twenty-first-century counterpart represents a step backwards: thousands of miners
claw ore out of the mud with their bare hands. Comparing
the new world to the old seems a necessary part of my trip.
So, before I turn south, it is to Bisiye that I resolve to
go next.

4

Meeting the colonel

Calculating the price of conflict minerals

THE SKY ABOVE GOMA is thick with pot-bellied cargo planes. They take off and land three or four times an hour so that there always appears to be an ageing Russian twin-prop whining unnervingly low over the town; gilded bees returning to a hive. The Bisiye tin mine is deep in the rainforest, near a town called Walikale. The road there has long since rotted away and so the only way to get there, or to get the tin ore out, is to fly over the crumbling road and rebel territory.

Tin is North Kivu's main export and Bisiye is responsible for two-thirds of the goods. But that's just the official number. Somewhere between the mine and the Rwandan border, most of the tin ore, worth four times North Kivu's reported export earnings, goes missing.

'Why do you want to go to Walikale?' asks Bonane, the charming immigration officer at Goma airport. 'Goma is nice, why not stay in Goma?'

My disingenuous cover story, which I explain to Bonane and his curious boss, is that I am an academic from the University of London, researching how the Congolese are surviving despite the war. I pull out a letter written by a friend, what is called in Congo an *ordre du mission*. I don't think they believe me but they eventually give me permission all the same.

Just as I am about to leave Bonane's plastic-panelled office, with its view over the runway, a junior official bursts into the room in floods of tears. He throws himself on the floor.

'I am sorry, sir, I am so sorry, my captain, I made a mistake. I won't do it again', he wails.

It seems the poor boy asked for a bribe from a white man who promptly reported him.

'Calm down, calm down', says Bonane, 'it's not a big deal. You just need to realize who you can ask and who you cannot'.

Bonane is understanding. The problem, he says to me, is not the stealing. The problem is that everyone acts like VIPs, jumping into their cars on the tarmac without passing through the terminal building. They treat the immigration officials as an annoyance, ignoring the formalities and reducing the chances for the staff to earn a little bonus.

'It's not like it used to be', he complains. 'Nowadays people have no respect for the authorities.'

An hour later I am peering through the scratched and dirty window of an ageing cargo plane, perched on a tiny slip of a seat. There does not appear to be a new plane in the country. Enormous trees, huts, people and several rusting carcasses of crashed aeroplanes rush past, very close, only just beyond the tips of the wings. And then, with a bump and a bounce, we are down. Behind me is two tonnes of dried fish. When the door opens I breathe deep, satisfying gulps of fresh air in the brilliant sunshine. A crowd swarms around the plane, unloading the fish, packing in tin, and spinning the plane by hand so it does a little pirouette on the narrow tarmac to face the other direction, ready for take-off again. Slowly, my nausea ebbs.

There are people living in huts all along the runway. I realize that's because it's not a runway at all, it is a road. Walikale used to have an airport but it is not in use any more, so would-be visitors must land on this, the only straight and metalled stretch of road around, and travel the remaining twenty-seven kilometres by motorbike. The edges of the road are cracked and ill-defined; in some places it's barely wide enough for the wheels of a twin-engine cargo plane. I can see why the forest along the roadside is littered with the burnt and twisted carcasses of planes. Otherwise it is the most impressive piece of tarmac I have yet seen in Congo.

As I step down from the plane I peer up into the cockpit and glimpse an old, scraggy, white pilot taking a shot of something. He gives me a slightly guilty grin and says 'Hah, welcome to Russia, cheers!' before knocking back another.

The town of Walikale straddles a bend in a wide brown river that flows in a steep gorge through thick forest. Squat houses huddle together on the edge of the gorge, peering down at the women bashing their laundry against the rocks below. A kind passer-by guides me across a bridge, towards the one hotel in Walikale town but then looks up and stops dead. Walking towards us is a man wearing spotless shoes and an ankle-length cream coat. He is flanked by several soldiers with guns over their shoulders. My guide steps to the side and slightly bows his head.

'*Bonjour, mon colonel. Je vous présente ...*' he begins but the colonel waves his hand hurriedly and absent-mindedly reaches to shake mine. His gaze is elsewhere, in the distance. Something in the jungle has his attention.

'We go to my house', says the colonel, and we fall in behind him.

My guide explains that this is Colonel Ibrahim, the military commander of the town. Now that I am in safe hands, he goes on, I will, of course, excuse him and, before I can say a word, he is gone.

Colonel Ibrahim's house has a little wooden fence, painted white, like a replica of the American Midwest. Keeping guard are three or four more soldiers. In a straw hut by the gate a little pot of ugali, the stiff porridge made from maize meal, the central African staple diet, is cooking atop three stones: it's the soldiers' lunch. The garden is laid to lawn but someone has planted flowers in pots outside the front door of the house. The house walls are made of corrugated iron and cotton curtains hang in the windows.

The colonel enters first and then all ten of his retinue follow, squeezing on to what clearly were once church pews, ranged around a sheet of plywood set balanced on some ammunition cases. The colonel disappears into another room. When he re-emerges he is wearing shorts and a baseball shirt and different, equally brilliantly white, spotless leather sandals.

A woman brings a large pot of ugali and fish and sets it down on the makeshift table. The colonel turns to me. 'White man, do you eat chilli?'

'Yes', I say.

'You're dangerous.'

Laughter all around the table, followed by a growl of 'Bismillahi', the Muslim grace, from the colonel. The assembled soldiers mumble 'Amin' but the word has barely passed their lips before large handfuls of ugali, dripping with sauce, are hastily shovelled in the opposite direction.

I manage two mouthfuls, then there is a shout from outside and the sound of rifles being cocked. Ibrahim is the first on his feet and out of the door. I peer through the window; several of the soldiers are holding two of their colleagues down on the grass while another cuts lengths of bamboo. Ibrahim takes off his nice clean shirt. The colonel shreds one bamboo cane on the back of one soldier and the other on the second. The pinned men scream for mercy in a babbled mash of French and Swahili. Apparently, they had cocked their rifles at each other in a fight over the little bowl of food.

After twenty solid minutes of beating, Colonel Ibrahim turns back to the house where his smiling wife awaits him with a towel. He disappears into the back room; when he emerges, his face is hot, his eyes wide and dilated from the rush of violence and he is sporting yet another freshly laundered t-shirt. He sits down roughly next to me and plunges his hand into the bowl of soup. I can see the beads of sweat on his closely-shaved skull.

'*Passeport.*' He jerks his chin in my direction.

My heart stops for a moment: I had been lulled into thinking all was well but this man is clearly capable of anything. Suddenly, the cute house looks sinister. The cluster of armed men with food dripping from their hands is not laughing anymore. I lay my passport on the table.

'*Ordre du mission?*'

I pull out my fake letter from the University of London.

'*Vaccination?*'

I give him my yellow fever certificate. He lays it on top of the rest, reads them all through once more, and pulls some fish bones from his teeth. There is a long silence during which I can only think that he wants me to understand that I am at his mercy, which of course I am. The soldiers continue shovelling food into their mouths but their eyes are fixed on the colonel. The hairs on my neck start to prickle.

'Welcome to Walikale. If you want to go to the mine we will protect you. If you want to stay in Walikale we will protect you. In fact, wherever you go, we will protect you.'

'Thank you.'

It sounds nice but the principal threat to my safety is probably from Ibrahim and his soldiers. After lunch he changes once again, this time into shorts and leather sandals that match his leather baseball cap. He walks me to the hotel in town, the one I had attempted to reach earlier. It is a simple concrete building with small dark rooms, owned by a large man in a slightly stained *kanzu*, the traditional Islamic tunic. There are stickers on the doors for backpacking organisations that date from the 70s and 80s.

'This is Shamis. He is my father in the church, because I am a Muslim', says the colonel.

'Yes, Allah be praised', says Shamis. He looks pleased: he has not had guests in a while. As the menacing colonel leaves, I breathe again.

Shamis is thrilled with his guest, especially one that speaks Swahili. I am treated to a sumptuous goat stew, tea from an enormous aluminium pot and a shouted conversation on the veranda as the rain thunders down. We discuss the history of the Swahili slave-trading networks that spread up from Lake Tanganyika across Congo. In his view, the slaving was a minor infraction; the Swahilis did Congo a service by bringing them Islam. When I need to go to the loo, and ask for a bowl of water rather than paper, he is beside himself:

'But you, you are a real Muslim! Water! Bring water!' he screams to his wife.

When I come out to breakfast in the morning, Shamis is dressed in a bright yellow three-piece suit.

'Is there a wedding?' I ask.

'Ha! No, there is a meeting of all the sultans of the district; one of the sultan-ships has become vacant.'

A legacy of the Swahili here is that some people still call chiefs by the Swahili name, Sultan. Shamis is one of them. Chiefs from far and wide have converged on Walikale, the district capital, and Shamis agrees to bring some to talk to me in the afternoon. Two come. One is called Mwami Nukonge Birunga *'le quatre'*, and the other simply Bamungu. They have chiefly titles but they are not in charge of their areas. A rebel group is. The Hutu *Forces démocratique pour la libération du Rwanda* control much of the district. The FDLR is made up of ex-Rwandan forces and the paramilitary Hutu *Interahamwe* that perpetrated the genocide before fleeing Rwanda back in 1994.

The enmity of the Rwandan genocide lives on in Congo; it is these Hutu militias that the rebel Tutsi general Laurent Nkunda claims to be fighting, because, he says, the Congolese army will not. In truth they probably cannot. Like a cancer, the FDLR has colonized North and South Kivu, enslaving the population and living on it. A large percentage of people in the east of Congo, especially those in the more remote areas, where the national army fears to tread, live under the dominion of the FDLR.

Birunga and Bamungu tell how they walked for three days to reach the meeting; their villages are over a hundred kilometres away through the bush, and the roads are long gone. They want me to return with them to see at first hand the system that the FDLR has established. The FDLR owns all the schools, hospitals, markets and shops and forces the people to work for them in the fields and in the mines. The FDLR elite takes all the crops and all the profits. Malnutrition is rife.

The FDLR has terrified the population so much that people will now only go to market in convoys. Up to one hundred people at a time walk through the forest guarded by the FDLR troops, who charge them for this protection. The previous month, Birunga's neighbour had refused to sleep with an FDLR commander. Her body was found two days later in the forest, mutilated and headless.

'They are repatriating the Congolese and Congo is still warring. But there has been peace in Rwanda for ten years now. Why are they not sending the FDLR back home?' Bamungu wants to know.

The point is that the FDLR don't want to go back to Rwanda. They have a lucrative life here mining ore and exploiting people and, after the unspeakable things some of them did in the genocide, they fear the justice of Paul Kagame, the new Tutsi president of Rwanda. Kagame has ruled Rwanda with an iron fist in the last fifteen years, driving economic development and eliminating threats to his authority with equal zeal. Disentangling the FDLR troops from their host population will be like uprooting bindweed.

A young man sporting neat clothes and a closely shaved head interrupts our interview on the porch.

'*Monsieur* Rawlence? I am afraid you must accompany me to the ANR office.'

The *Agence national de renseignements* (ANR) is the Congolese national intelligence agency. So far I have avoided any run-ins with them, but they are notoriously difficult. Shamis leaps to his feet, six feet of shimmering yellow suit bearing down on the poor little man.

'What is the meaning of this? The *monsieur* is our guest!'

'Foreigners are not permitted in Walikale. The *monsieur* is to leave immediately', he insists.

The sultans whip out their mobile phones like knives and for a moment I think they are going to strike the man with them. But all their pleading with their various contacts within the bureaucracy cannot shift the ANR. I would love to stay longer in Walikale; I had hoped to go to the mine with Ibrahim and visit the sultans' villages. But the ANR has other plans.

The sultans are outraged. They shout at the poor officer, no more than a boy really, who has come to take me away.

'They do not want us to develop', says Bamungu.

'They do not want the outside world to know of our suffering', cries Birunga the fourth.

'We always blame the white man for bringing the war and now one of them comes here to find out what our problems are and we send him away? We don't help ourselves', says Shamis, with a sorry shake of the head.

He has been a generous host and I am very sorry to say goodbye.

In a little office made of breezeblocks, one half of which is ringed with yellow and black tape announcing DANGER – MINES, a droopy man in a bad suit chain-smokes cigarettes. He politely informs me that my stay here in Walikale is not authorized, whatever the nice immigration officer Bonane may have said. He won't explain but I suspect someone has heard that I'm interested in the mine, and it's in no one's interest that the full story of the riches of Bisiye should be told.

I am confined in this office. Chickens scratch around outside and the mist lifts off the banana plantation on the hill above. Finally, the younger man returns with a borrowed motorbike and escorts me to the road where the planes land. We arrive back at the 'airport' just as the last plane of the day is being spun around by twenty pairs of hands. Everyone is screaming for money. The engines start and I push dollars into several different hands, I don't know whose, but it seems to work, and I am lifted and bundled into the hold of the plane, my bag is thrown in after me and the door slammed shut.

I sit up and collect myself. Outside the window the greens of the forest are a steady blur. Inside, the hold is empty, or so it seems. Then I count forty dirty plastic bags tied with string and arranged in four neat rows in the middle of the hold. They don't fill even a quarter of the plane but they are heavy: two tonnes of tin ore. For two days, each fifty-kilo bag has been carried on someone's head down a slippery track through the forest from the mine, and taxed many times on the way. People die for this stuff. These dirty bags in their neat rows comprise a significant piece of the conflict economy; they keep the war smouldering, like a forest fire that goes underground and re-surfaces at a later, unexpected date. Tin, and the works at Manono, were once a source of hope for Congo, but today these pitiful bags are a source of danger.

'Colonel Ibrahim? That guy's a fucking son of a bitch!' says Brian.

A few days later. Brian and I are sitting in his garden by the lake in Goma, drinking beers and watching the calm lake turn from silver to gold in the afternoon light. Brian is a South African businessman with a quick tongue. I have come to ask him about the tin trade at Bisiye, to understand how it works. He should know. His company holds what it believes to be the rights to the tin mine but the law has yet to reach Walikale. Three days before he thrashed two of his men in front of me, Ibrahim had threatened to spill Brian's blood all over the Bisiye mine.

The same gang has been in control of Walikale for years. Before they were given uniforms and a regular supply of ammunition, the 85th Brigade of the Congolese army, under the command of Colonel Ibrahim and Colonel Sammy, was a brutal Mai Mai rebel militia.

The Mai Mai were originally formed in the late 1990s, as a kind of home guard to assist the overstretched Congolese army, the *Forces armées de la République Démocratique du Congo* (FARDC), in their efforts to repel the many invaders of the second war. Chief among them was the repackaged rebel group, funded and organized by Rwanda, the *Rassemblement Congolais pour la démocratie* (RCD). The RCD and its various factions controlled Goma and most of the east for the much of the next decade. The Mai Mai saw themselves as nationalists but were generally armed thugs in the service of local warlords, who used insecurity as an opportunity for extortion, rape and plunder. Since the 2006 elections, various Mai Mai groups had begun to be 'integrated' into the national army, a process that in most cases involved some basic training, the promise of a regular salary and hefty pay-offs to the commanders.

The 85th Brigade was not yet integrated into the amorphous mass that made up the official FARDC. But, Brian said, even if they left Walikale, control of what is now Congo's largest tin mine would probably pass to another brigade and that gang would be just as reluctant to give it up.

Brian's company has a mandate to carry out 'research' at the mine. The problem for him and his team is that by the time they have established the viability of the mine, there will probably be nothing left in the ground. The state, meanwhile, insists that the company's permit is for 'research', not extraction. The officials have a point but in Congo the law is only one bargaining arrow in your quiver. The usual tools of wartime – men and guns – are the deciding factor in most business arrangements and the colonel has the most in the region. Sammy and Ibrahim and their gang are making a fortune.

Brian makes rough calculations in my notebook as we talk.

The soldiers don't themselves mine. Instead, they control the ten thousand to fifteen thousand miners who live and work in the muddy warrens of Bisiye. The soldiers levy a ten per cent tax on goods going up the mountain, and ten per cent on the tin ore that comes down, as well as charging a two-hundred-dollar fee for every aircraft that takes off from the tarmac road transporting rocks to Goma. There are between fifteen and twenty-four flights a day, each carrying two tonnes of material. Two or three days a month there is a kind of public holiday, a *salongo*. On those days, the military have decreed, all the tin produced at the mine belongs to them. By Brian's reckoning, Ibrahim and Sammy are netting a minimum of ten thousand dollars a day.

Everything at the mine is denominated in tin. Even sex: prostitutes working the miners charge twenty to fifty kilos of ore for a night.

Brian and his team are convinced that senior Congolese military commanders in Goma and Kinshasa are also garnering hefty cuts of the profits from the Walikale mine. Peace would mean the unwelcome attention of the government, the advent of commercial mining operations, taxation and the end of their private income. In such circumstances, organized industrial mining, of the kind that made Manono rich and colonial Congo famous, at present makes no sense for a multi-national company like Brian's.

'The real problem', says Brian with a sigh, 'is that war is good for business, just not ours'.

5

Guerrillas in the mist

Transporting bags of charcoal in Virunga National Park

THE LAST PIECE OF the conflict puzzle that J-B wants me to see before he will allow me on my way to Manono is the FDLR, the militia that is causing such havoc for the sultans around Walikale. The FDLR controls large swathes of rural Kivu and makes money from mining, poaching, smuggling and extortion. There's a unit not far from J-B's radio station. He has wanted to go and visit them for a while and he thinks having a white man along would be just the bait he needs to get an interview. He tells me to be at the government offices at nine sharp.

I walk up the hill towards the square white office of the governor and meet a crowd swarming down the street in the other direction. It seems to be a protest about corruption, a vain and noble undertaking in Congo. In the wake of the crowd, I spy a grinning J-B waving at me from the passenger seat of a black saloon car with smoky windows. The car has an excellent sound system and is driven by a truculent man called Lambé. Rutshuru, where J-B runs the Racou FM radio station, is about half-way to the unit's camp; we will stop and say hello. The road that far is good, but beyond there it gets worse, and it's raining. Our main problem is not going to be finding the FDLR but whether Lambé's pretty car can get us there at all.

The smooth tarmac road rises gently north from Goma, between the twin peaks of the volcanoes of Virunga National Park, made famous by Dian Fossey and *Gorillas in the Mist*. We pass an old metal sign for the park, swaying on a fence post: it is a sieve of bullet holes. Behind it, some park rangers are sitting on the porch, polishing their guns. The joke in Goma is that, unlike the Congolese army, the rangers actually use their weapons. Their smart new vehicles and their intact uniforms are testament to the international money that comes in to protect the gorillas of the park.

After a short while we pull up at a roadblock. A tree has been stripped of its branches and hauled across the road and a beanpole soldier, with a rifle bouncing on his hip, pokes his face through the passenger window.

'Should I pretend that I am rich, that my children are not hungry, that I don't need your assistance?' he asks, his face splitting with pleasure at his audacity. Two other soldiers stand at the roadside, watching us uneasily.

J-B reaches into a fraying laptop case and pulls out a notepad, his tape recorder, some old tissues, until he finds what he is looking for: a jumbo pack of condoms.

'I can't give you money', he says to the soldier, 'but I can give you life. Take care!' He pushes a fistful of condoms into the soldier's hand. For a moment the frown on the soldier's face tightens and I think he might slap or shoot J-B for his impertinence. But then he relaxes into a grin, shakes his head, and wags his finger at us. He motions for the two other soldiers to drag the tree trunk to one side, just enough for us to inch past and then roar off.

Beyond the roadblock a white pick-up has broken down. On its side is the logo of the national park; several armed rangers are standing around on the verge. At their feet three girls, very dirty, are crying and screaming, their grubby bodies shaking heavily with their sobs. I ask them what's wrong.

'They don't speak Swahili. Rwandan, they are', says one of the rangers to me, laughing.

The girls had emerged from the bush carrying large loads of charcoal at the exact spot where the park rangers' car had broken down and they were changing a wheel. Two girls had tried to run away but the rangers gave chase and dragged them back. Burning trees to make charcoal is a major problem in the national park and is officially illegal.

It is illegal in Rwanda too but, unlike Congo, in Rwanda the ban is enforced. So hundreds of poor Rwandan children are sent over the border into Congo to try to make a living.

One ranger is standing guard while the girls pull at their hair with blackened hands and wail hysterically in Kinyarwanda. They don't seem to be pleading with their captors. I suspect they know it won't make any difference. Rather, the sound is mournful, as though someone has died, as if they are grieving for their own misfortune. The more the girls wail, the more the rangers laugh.

'They should be afraid', says J-B. 'If they do arrest them, the rangers have no sympathy for Rwandans.'

'What can we do?' I ask J-B.

'Nothing. It happens every day, and they have broken the law', he says.

It's terrifying to think what these rangers might do to these poor young girls if they get them alone in custody. The incidence of rape in eastern Congo is the highest in the world. It's not just a weapon of war but a consequence of the general lawlessness and impunity. You're never likely to be brought to book for abusing a young girl, nor even for killing one. You can get away with anything.

It's not even clear what the law means in such a context. For these young girls however, the law is the armed men standing over them and it's not to be argued with. As we get back into the car, in an ironic insult to their wretchedness, a huge truck piled high with charcoal thunders past, with several Congolese army soldiers clinging to the back.

I begin to notice, all along the road, every hundred yards or so, paths beaten into the bush where a soldier or two stands guard. They are stationed to collect bribes from the Rwandan villagers as they leave the national park with their illegal charcoal and head for the border. Unluckily for the girls, they had met well-paid rangers who actually care about the park and do their job. Charcoal is big business for the Congolese soldiers, who supplement their paltry wages with the bribes. The FDLR, which practises logging on a much larger scale, also makes big money from the park. Blood charcoal.

The rain has stopped and the clouds lift to reveal steep green slopes rising above us on three flanks, and plains, gold and green in the morning sun, rolling gently north towards the Rwandan border. The tops of the volcanoes are in the clouds but plumes of smoke rise steadily from the forest, curling reminders of the ever-present destruction. The thick green seems so huge it must be hard for the charcoal burners to imagine the end of the forest, to picture the plains to the north stretching all the way to the volcanoes, but if unchecked, that is what the landscape will become.

The sides of the road are thick with the protected forest, from which emerge boys and girls, children, pushing home-made wooden wheelbarrows brimming with charcoal. Around one corner, in among the dirty kids, we come across two tall well-dressed women with a different cargo, carrying a mattress on their heads. Following behind are several kids holding plastic buckets packed tight with cooking utensils. Further on more appear, then more, and suddenly the road is clogged with people carrying their possessions on their heads and we have to stop the car.

J-B asks an old man with a walking stick what's going on. Nkunda's forces had been spotted in the bush nearby yesterday, so the villagers are walking to Goma rather than waiting to see what atrocities his soldiers will commit this time. These refugees will add to the multitudes in Goma's refugee camps and stay indefinitely, unsure when it will be safe to return home: a life lived in fear, ruled by rumours. J-B wants to know what they have seen and heard, so he can broadcast it today. He is also worried that if Nkunda is around it means the FDLR is likely to have made itself scarce.

Rutshuru sits on the edge of a hill, overlooking the plains beneath the cloud-shrouded volcanoes. It is a pretty town, ruined by soldiers. The FARDC has flooded the place: soldiers walk along the road with rocket-propelled grenades casually slung over their shoulders and lounge in the market smoking cigarettes, feet up on 12-mm machine guns, belts of ammunition on the ground. Rutshuru is J-B's home town and Racou FM his baby. We pull up in front of a two-storey concrete building by the river and ascend some iron steps on the outside of the building.

'Welcome to the tallest building in Rutshuru!' shouts J-B. Inside is a huge table, around which reporters are preparing the news in Racou's official languages: French, Nandi, Swahili and English. J-B's managerial style seems to consist of handing out condoms, cracking a few jokes and leaving. The shabby building belies Racou's importance as one of the few sources of independent news in the war zone. Its antenna, bending in the wind, may be the tallest thing in Rutshuru, but it is still not tall enough for all those who want to listen. There are hundreds of thousands of people within the sixty-mile radius of Racou's broadcast but thousands more beyond without the benefit of J-B's well-connected sources. Here, such titbits of information can be the difference between life and death.

Racou's value lies in its independence, which in large part is down to the personal bravery of J-B and his staff. They must negotiate a complex network of shifting political alliances, remaining close enough to the military groups to get information but maintaining enough distance not to become co-opted. Offending the militias on air can have deadly consequences; J-B spends much of his time placating military commanders and fighting to keep the station open. The rebel, Rwandan-backed RCD administration repeatedly tried to shut down Racou. Life between Nkunda, Rwanda's new proxy, and the Congolese army is not much easier. Shortly after my visit, one of Racou's reporters was shot in the street by unknown gunmen.

The road out of town takes us past the trenches of the Congolese army, where soldiers sit on plastic jerry cans outside green tents, listening to their radios. They wear regulation uniforms with green wellington boots, which rest in the shallow muddy trenches that are more like drains than something one could hide in. They wave warily at us as we glide past in the pimped-up car. They are nervously awaiting Nkunda's rumoured offensive. Down the road we curve past a bombed-out post office shadowed by a spooky dead tree and pass ranks of trucks parked in the lee of a pretty bougainvillea-covered villa being used by the military command.

A few kilometres out of town we find an abandoned FDLR camp by the road. It looks fresh: the leaves thatching the huts are still green in places and plastic bowls lie overturned, as though the soldiers had left in a hurry. A woman passes by with a bucket of water on her head; when J-B asks her where they have gone, she tips her chin in the direction of the road ahead.

The rains have churned the tracks into deep gorges that Lambé must navigate with two wheels on the verge. The road is indeed our main obstacle; we proceed at a painful pace. After an hour or so we notice a boy, very young-looking, wearing a military uniform and clutching a rifle, who rather unsuccessfully tries to hide behind a tree when we approach. J-B rolls down the window.

'Get in the car and take us to your commander', he barks.

To my astonishment, the boy clambers in beside me, resting his gun between his knees. The car crawls along the road. After another half an hour an older man, in sunglasses, tracksuit and wellington boots, steps out into the middle of the road and points his gun at the car.

'Wish me luck', says J-B.

He explains to the man with the gun that we want to speak to his boss. The soldier looks uncertain for a moment then pulls out a phone, dials a number, and speaks rapidly in Kinyarwanda. He passes the phone to J-B, who breaks into a wide smile as he speaks.

'*Bonjour, mon colonel ...*'

Success. There are now two soldiers with AK-47s in the back of the car, one on either side of me. I watch the barrels swinging lazily between their legs, pointing up at my head. Lambé has a pained expression on his face as the car crunches from one bump to the next. He looks relieved when, after about three kilometres, another soldier steps from behind some coffee bushes and into the road. With his rifle he first motions for us to park the car and then points at a bench.

The three of us perch uneasily on the bench, beneath a pink bougainvillea rioting all over the side of a pretty little mud house. The courtyard is swept and a pair of wellington boots stands on the ground just by the front door. The next house is the same: immaculate, separated by a low clipped hedge cut into a perfect square shape. The roofs are tin and the window frames are wood, neatly jointed in small squares. Across the road coffee bushes are arranged in tidy lines stretching away down the hill.

So this is what rebel territory looks like, I think to myself.

The order of it is strangely sinister, and I remember that many of the FDLR were those who carried out the genocide in cold and clinical fashion. J-B is confident and chatty but my heart is in my mouth. I am not so sure that his idea of using me as bait to get an interview was such a good one.

From one of the delicate little houses steps another soldier, carrying two rifles. He tells us to follow him. In a slightly larger house, with hand-embroidered net curtains at the windows, three men sit around a table. One portly man in a photographer's jacket, another in a string vest in Rasta colours, and another in pinstripe trousers, pressed shirt, pointy shoes and an enormous felt cowboy hat. He is Rachid, the colonel.

Rachid has a small sliver of a moustache, which he fingers as he talks. He fires a round of questions at us, then pauses, stroking his moustache and flexing the pointy ends of his shoes, pretending to deliberate on whether to grant us an interview. The performance doesn't last long; Colonel Rachid is angry, and he wants to vent.

'The FDLR have given us refugees from Rwanda a bad name. All they are interested in is making money', he fumes.

'But are you not the FDLR'? I ask.

'No. We were. We have formed a new group, *Raillement pour l'unité et la démocratie*, RUD, those of us who are truly committed to returning to Rwanda and over-throwing the dictator, Kagame.'

According to Rachid, the FDLR are using 'unconventional logistics', exploiting Congo and its people. They have forgotten their original goal of returning to Rwanda. Now they only want to make money mining gold, diamonds and tourmaline, and taxing the people of Congo so that they can live well. They have discovered that colonial occupation pays: life for them in Rwanda would be difficult, compared to the luxury of Congo. And so, despite the various offers of amnesty and deadlines for return to Rwanda, they stay, parasites, he says, on their Congolese hosts. It is nice to hear him confirming what critics of the FDLR say all the time. Of course, he says, his RUD is different; it is committed to military discipline and protecting the civilians of Congo.

'Look at this village? Do these people look oppressed to you?' he asks with a wave of his hand.

I don't know what to say, and J-B just laughs. I dig him in the ribs; we don't want to upset this man while surrounded by teenagers holding rifles. Until very recently, Rachid and his men were just like the rest of the FDLR, stopping the traffic on the road from Uganda, demanding one dollar for pedestrians, two dollars for a motorbike, a portion of any goods being transported and up to twenty dollars from the trucks that bring petrol to Goma. Now, things have changed, he says; he doesn't take any tax and his men live well alongside the Congolese in this village. His children go to Congolese schools and are learning Swahili. He and his men 'collaborate' with the civilians, taking a percentage of their harvest.

'Many of my men have inter-married with the Congolese, so how could they be accused of oppressing them?' he protests.

He calls for his wife and children to illustrate his point. They file in one by one, in freshly laundered white and blue frilly dresses and sparkly plastic shoes, stepping gingerly over the rifles by the door. There are four girls, the two smallest ones wearing lipstick and with kohl smudged round their eyes, like dolls, and an infant boy whom Rachid holds aloft and shakes in my direction.

'A son!' he shouts, as though this one is more important than all the others.

Despite what he says about wishing to go home to Rwanda, life looks pretty good for him here. The family is well fed, fat even. They look happy and relaxed. When we stand outside the house and line up to have our picture taken together, the boys pose with their rifles and Rachid with his son. During the whole visit we meet none of the Congolese Hutus who slave in the fields only to have their crops appropriated. I'd like to see if they look so fat and content.

Afterwards, the captain in the string vest pulls me to one side.

'Do I look old enough to be a *génocidaire* to you?' he asks. Like many of the Hutu boys who fled Rwanda after the genocide, he fears being prosecuted for what happened. He says he was only seventeen at the time, too young to kill anyone. Seventeen seems old enough to me but I say nothing.

'Tell the world we are innocent', he pleads. 'We want to go home but we don't want to go to jail.' Ahh, I think: the nub of the issue. Colonel Rachid wants us to take his complaint to the international media; he wants the world to hear his side of the story.

'I am tired of the lies of the BBC', he says.

As we say our goodbyes, I look around for J-B and clock him off to one side, talking quietly with Rachid's oldest daughter. She is sixteen and studying in Rwanda. Back in the car, I tease him.

'Are you nuts? Did you want to get us killed, laughing at that maniac and trying to sleep with his daughter?'

'Calm down, I may be reckless, but I am not a fool', he says. 'The poor girl wanted condoms. She fears her father's men might rape her at any time.'

Returning to Rutshuru, we are overtaken by a motorbike. Perched on the back is a woman with a brown sack wrapped awkwardly around her waist. The FDLR, RUD, or whatever they call themselves, may have given up on roadblocks but not on poaching; in that sack is another ready source of income, an antelope on its way to Rutshuru market, where these days its meat is cheaper than goat. There are no hippos left in Lake Edward, because the FDLR poached them all in what one of the rangers told me was 'an almost industrial destruction of the hippo population'. At one point last year a whole hippo went for fifty dollars: cheaper than beef.

It's late. We won't make it back to Goma tonight so J-B suggests we stop and visit his mother in Rutshuru. We surprise her; she hasn't enough food for three extra mouths so she sends a cousin out into the night. The girl returns a short while later with 'FDLR meat'. Poached bushmeat: probably that antelope. J-B's mum apologizes but what can she do? She buys what the market provides, and 'fair trade' meat, so to speak, is increasingly expensive.

We have brought beer. While the antelope grills we sit in the low concrete house on orange velour sofas. On the wall, next to a photo of a slim J-B surrounded by lots of beautiful female relatives, is a small silver crucifix. J-B gives his mum a beer, which she takes into her own room, and he tells the story of the time when some of the rangers from the national park came to the radio station and read out on air a list of people they knew were poaching, warning them to stop. The FDLR was incensed and took the station hostage. The soldiers read out their own declaration, ending 'Would you rather we ate animals or you people?'

Some of the rangers are in direct competition with the FDLR for control of the poaching market, which is why they threatened them on Racou FM. The FDLR charges poachers thirty dollars in protection fees to allow them to hunt in the park but the rangers demand a hundred. Not so clean after all. If even the rangers are on the make, I will be surprised if there are any animals left in the park in five years' time.

After a while J-B's mum emerges from her room wearing a different outfit and with slightly wider, glassy eyes. She has drunk the whole half-litre bottle of Primus in one go.

'She always does that', says J-B, 'then continues as if nothing has happened, hah-hah!'

6

Blood cheese

Herding cows in North Kivu

ON MY LAST DAY in Goma, with time to kill, I go shopping. Near the market is a shop with a crumbling concrete facade. Harried workers are making baguettes at two dollars a go for Goma's lunchtime rush whilst in a refrigerated cabinet along one side sit dozens of round black cylinders, like landmines.

'What's that?' I ask the shop assistant in Swahili.

'*Fromage de Goma*', she replies in prim French.

I buy one, a whole one, for myself. I love cheese but it was the last thing I expected to find in Goma. I intend to eat all of it. It's like a Gouda; in my eagerness to cram the hard waxy slices into my mouth I almost forget to wonder: who on earth makes cheese in a place like this? The fighting that everyone feared, and that the refugees from Rutshuru anticipated, has just broken out. Nkunda's forces and the Congolese army are clashing outside the town. Where does this stuff come from?

On the back of the waxy rind is a roughly printed label bearing a mobile phone number. I call it, and that is how I meet Eugene and discover the cows of Kivu's conflict economy. Eugene isn't surprised at my phone call; in fact he is delighted to meet someone taking an interest in his business. He suggests we meet that afternoon at one of the smart hotels overlooking the lake.

Eugene is a softly spoken man with rimless glasses and intelligent eyes. He is the biggest cheese producer in North Kivu and is exactly my age. Armed with a ready smile, he laughs at all my questions.

'How do you make cheese in a war zone?'

'To a large extent the war is about cows – and grazing', he says.

Eugene explains that while the proceeds from mining, poaching and smuggling sustain the more recent eruptions of fighting and, to some extent, have become their cause, North Kivu has long been the site of tensions over land and ethnicity. The hills of Masisi were once forested, like those further west at Walikale, but now they look like Switzerland, complete with milkers.

'Cattle ranching is the biggest industry in this area. The cows are at the centre of the conflict, it is a goal of the war to secure land for the cows. But while the herds and the fields may change sides, the cows still produce milk, whomever they belong to.'

Eugene was studying business management at the institute in Goma just as the first war was breaking out. His family is Hutu and his father was a cattle rancher caught up in the fighting. Eugene looked for a business that would be above politics, above the fighting and that could thrive whoever owned the cows. He hit on cheese.

Leading politicians and military commanders on both sides of the conflict own the cows that Eugene needs to make his cheese. He buys milk from them all. He employs twenty people and runs three cheese factories, although two are currently out of action.

'There is no shortage of milk, and when it rains there is even more milk. The only problem is that the fighting causes the cattle to move away from my *fromageries*.' Refugee cows.

If milk is such big business, then it must contribute significant funds to the belligerents on both sides. A single cow can produce up to one hundred litres a day: eight thousand Congolese francs, about forty dollars. Even in the currently depressed climate, Eugene's business consumes up to six hundred litres of milk a day; $7200 a month for the owners of the cows, the majority of them warlords, politicians or financiers of the conflict in one way or other.

At full capacity he would use ten times as much, and Eugene is only one producer.

'So, in a way, your cheese is helping fuel the conflict? In the same way that conflict diamonds are called blood diamonds, we could call your cheese "blood cheese"?' I ask him with a cheeky smile.

He smiles, too, and, leaning back, draws his arm in an arc towards the lake.

'What do you see?'

From the hotel on the lake where we are having coffee we can see houses glittering behind tall walls that but for the razor wire, would not look out of place on the French Riviera. The contrast with the dark of the lake is sharp. The thick black water, quietly knocking at the bottom of the gardens, is a gentle reminder of the peril just below the surface of everything in Goma. The water is full of deadly gas yet this is some of the most expensive property in Africa. The landlords have a captive market in the UN peacekeepers and international agency workers stationed in Goma. The going rate for these lakeside palaces is five thousand dollars a month, or more, and there are not enough to meet demand. Many UN staff live in hotels while awaiting accommodation or on temporary contracts.

Eugene gently points out that all those villas, all the petrol stations, truck companies, this hotel, belong to warlords with ties to different militias or to the Congolese army. Nothing has really changed. The UN peacekeepers are the biggest customers in town for villas and petrol and vehicles. They are pumping the most money into Goma's economy, which keeps all these armed groups in business.

'I am not into politics', he says. 'I am just a businessman. You cannot make or trade anything in Congo that does not somehow put money in the wrong hands.' Eugene is right. Every movement in the militarized economy of North Kivu greases the wheels of conflict. This prosperous, fertile province, with industry and universities that were the envy of Africa in the 1950s and 60s, has become a gilded circle of hell.

7

'The waves on the lake are not negligible, my dear'

Money changers in the street market, Bukavu

IT IS EARLY IN the morning when J-B and Lambé drop me at the ferry the next day. It is time to go south from Goma to Lake Tanganyika and beyond to Manono, to voyage into what should be comparatively peaceful territory, although no one really knows what is going on down there. First, I must cross another lake, Lake Kivu, to the city of Bukavu.

J-B has given me the name of one person who has been south of Uvira, the town that sits at the head of Lake Tanganyika and the place I must reach next: a radio journalist called Dupont who lives in Bukavu. Dupont sometimes visits the main towns down the lake but he does it in a plane. When I emailed him about the possibility of a boat that could take me to visit the villages between the towns on the lake shore, he simply wrote back, 'the waves on the lake are not negligible, my dear'. Translated, he meant, 'Don't be an idiot'. For the last few days I have been calling him but his phone is off.

The sky is low and cold, like steel. There is a wind up and the lake is choppy and grey. Down a steep hill is a small cove hemmed in by sharp cliffs, at the base of which sit several abandoned containers and a rusty shed: the ticket office.

'I've got a present for you', says J-B.

He puts a condom in my hand and bursts out laughing.

'No, seriously', he says and gives me a small plastic bag.

Inside is a t-shirt printed with a photo of Joseph Kabila: 'Lil' Joseph', as J-B likes to call him. The boyish and stylish president could easily pass for an American rapper with his white suits and bejewelled hands. The t-shirt is a souvenir of the 2006 election campaign, which Lil' Joseph won with the slogan: *Votez Kabila pour un Congo fort et prospère.*

The very thought of strength, of prosperity may be a distant dream to most Congolese living in this moment and the president may have little idea how to bring about such a dream. But at least in 2006 he captured the desires of his people, along with their votes. His next electoral outing, in 2011, having created neither strength nor prosperity, was a much tougher affair; people wanted more than simply peace, they wanted to see some progress, and Kabila rigged the vote heavily.

At the other side of Lake Kivu, waiting outside the ferry terminal in Bukavu, as though put there just for me, is a single taxi. It is owned by Alain.

Alain drives me to three different Christian missions looking for a bed for the night but they are all full. As he manoeuvres his clean white car through the mud of Bukavu he bemoans the awful roads. We listen to his favourite tape of Pentecostal Christian songs performed by the choir from his church. I ask if he has any bolingo music.

'No. I am preparing myself, and the tapes help. You should do the same', he advises.

Alain thinks that all the elements for the second coming of the Messiah are in place: war, hunger, strife. But this has been true for hundreds of years; millenarianism of one form or another has a long history in the great lakes. From the eighteenth century until the 1930s, the cult of Nyabinghi drew followers with a similar idea of impending spiritual transcendence. In these hills bordering Rwanda,

Uganda and Congo, a religious sect emerged in which women possessed by a spirit became priestesses and ruled in a matriarchal fashion. It was Nyabinghi priestesses, Muhumusa the most famous among them, who led the Kiga tribes against imperial armies at the turn of the twentieth century, prophesying the end of the world. They eventually lost to the British (in Uganda), the Germans (in Tanzania) and the Belgians (in Rwanda and Congo). In many ways their prophesy was true: the Belgian occupation of the Congo, the decimation of its population at the hands of rubber planters – who chopped off workers' hands to encourage greater production – can only be viewed as apocalyptic. And then came the wars, with Rwanda, the rebels, each other.

I tell Alain that if Judgement Day is coming then he needn't worry about the road, or about my fare for that matter. At this he gets very serious.

'No! We must fix the road! If we stop caring about the road, then we are already dead'.

The name Bukavu means 'the place of few people'. Now it is the largest city in the east of the country, bigger than Goma and the capital of South Kivu province, North Kivu's equally miserable sibling. The town is arranged on a series of fingers that stick out into the lake like a hand spread wide. The main harbour is in the gap between the thumb and forefinger. Houses are crammed together precipitously on each of the fingers, craning for a view of the lake.

Down a long avenue at the end of one of the fingers sits the *Centre d'Amani*, the peace centre, a Catholic mission.

Alain pleads with the *curé* on my behalf and he grants me a bed. Since Dupont's phone remains off, and my way south remains unclear, Alain takes me to the two places I want to see in town.

First stop is the former presidential palace of Mobutu, called '*le boat*' because it sits, surrounded by water, on the most prominent finger. The plinths on the gateposts are empty, the garden is planted with maize and soldiers live in its echoing rooms.

The second is the *Musée geologique*. On the main street in Bukavu the 1950s concrete block of the geological museum is a monument to a more hopeful past. Inside are beautifully made glass cabinets containing every single kind of rock found in Congo. There are many: an almost complete geological survey of the Earth. Small typed labels and handwritten numbers describe the displays, although, here and there, cases have been broken and specimens have been lost. At one end of the room is a dusty case with human bones and worked prehistoric stones. A small round grey rock, flecked with amethyst, offers, in French, a little clue for me on my treasure hunt: '*Etain, Manono*'. Tin, Manono.

Outside, a tall old man with a long white beard, a shabby suit and spectacles sits on the step. He is the director. He has been in charge for ten years without drawing a salary but he stays on. He considers the work to be his calling.

'I am sorry for the state of the museum', he says. 'Come again! Next time it will be fixed up, next time!'

A column of schoolchildren are marching up the street towards us, led by two female teachers. The children are wearing a uniform of white shirts tucked into maroon skirts or shorts and are holding hands in pairs. The director excuses himself, for he must give them a tour. It is, he explains, his duty to pass on his knowledge of the geological riches of Congo to the next generation.

'After all, it will be up to them to use our national wealth to make Congo strong once more!'.

The Amani centre's church, dormitories and twin quadrangles occupy their own peninsula. I take a moment's silence in the little chapel and contemplate my venture south into the unknown. A nun comes in and sits down silently next to me and when I leave she is still there, head down.

Afterwards, I stroll around the headland on an immaculate gravel path, passing through eucalyptus trees, bamboo groves and bushes of huge white flowers whose name I don't know. Another nun passes me as I rest on a bench. She smiles, points to a small landing stage through the trees and makes a swimming motion with her arms, then bows her head and is gone. I'm not sure if it's an order or a suggestion but since the nuns are vowed to silence I cannot ask her. I follow her instruction and go down to the wooden jetty, strip off and lower myself down the metal ladder into the cool clear water of the lake. I swim out and look back at the view of Bukavu, shining in the afternoon light. It must be one of the most beautiful settings for a city anywhere.

Around the point of the peninsula comes a line of fishing boats. I hear them before I see them. The fishermen are singing to themselves a low, slightly melancholy, tune in a minor key. It's a sad song that floats over the smooth surface of the lake interspersed with the chop-swoosh-chop of their paddles. With their long arched poles bent over the hulls, the boats look like huge water-boatmen with enormous feet skipping across the surface tension of the lake. Their song is interrupted by another sound, the far-off tinkle of the bell calling the silent nuns to prayer.

My prayers centre on Dupont's telephone but they, and the phone, remain unanswered. I cannot wait for someone who may not arrive, so I resolve to simply follow my nose south to the next lake, Lake Tanganyika. Alain accompanies me to Tel Aviv, Bukavu's hottest club, for my last night and we dance to the devil's bolingo music until way beyond his bedtime.

In the morning Alain drops me at the bus station and leaves me sleepily waiting for the bus to Uvira while he goes back to his angry wife and to bed.

'I love you', he says in English when he goes.

The bus pulls out along the top of the ridge and then drops down to the border post with Rwanda on the lake, passing the disabled people ferrying maize flour across the border on makeshift bicycle wheelchairs. They are exempted from taxes and so enjoy a monopoly on the trade between the border posts. It is a kind of structural economic welfare programme.

The bus thunders through the green hills of Rwanda, because the road on the Congolese side is only a memory. Finally, it crosses the Ruzizi River and rejoins Congo on the plains beneath the mountains that tower above the lake. The road crests a small rise and the horizon is flooded with blue. This is the view I had from Bujumbura – the eastern border of Congo, the western shore of Lake Tanganyika, the gateway to the south. South Kivu province and then Katanga, beyond, is somewhere down that green and jagged shoreline, an emerald atop a sapphire, shining in the morning sun.

8

Outsiders

The Uvira car wash

THE CONGOLESE TOWN OF Uvira sits at the northern end of Lake Tanganyika, Africa's longest and deepest lake. Sharp green hills hang menacingly over the town like a line of broken glass bottles. The mountains, as high as the Alps, though snowless and now pretty much treeless, have had many names over the years but are currently known as the Mulenge range. This is where the pressures under Africa's Great Rift Valley have found their most dramatic expression. From the tips of the mountains to the floor of the lake is over four thousand metres of almost sheer drop.

Pushed up against the hills by the lake, Uvira has grown lengthways in the space between. Tin roofs dot the hillside but its main artery is the road that runs along the lakeshore. Anything that happens in the town happens here.

On the bright morning of my arrival, a church meeting has spilled over into the road. Trucks have been driven into the river to be washed, alongside hundreds of children, men, women and clothes. The bus station is also the road: minibuses sit along the roadside with little signs in the windows bearing the hand-written names of far-off towns. Stitching the scene together, goats weave in and out, stopping traffic like insouciant girls.

In the courtyard of a small concrete hotel recommended by Dupont, I dial his number one last time and, miracle, he answers! What's more, he is in Uvira this morning, staying in the same hotel. At this point he's the only person I know who's been further south. His being here is a godsend. I sit down to wait for the elusive man.

From his formal French and austere, disapproving tone, I had imagined someone tall, old and possibly grey; so I am surprised when a short smiling man seats himself at my table and announces with a giggle, '*Monsieur* Ben, I presume?'

I am so pleased to see him. He is a voluble man with an infectious smile, dressed in smart trainers and a freshly pressed, cheerful purple shirt; he is eager to help but remains unconvinced by my plan.

'But why? What is your job? What is your mission?'

He does not consider wandering around eastern Congo to be a serious proposition. Unless you have to.

'I want to see how people are coping after the war. I want to travel to the villages down the lake that you can't reach by road, that nobody hears about.' I try again. 'And after that, to go inland, to Manono.'

'Manono?' he says with a disbelieving laugh just like J-B's, although he is more polite. 'There, you must surely fly.'

He raises an eyebrow and shakes his head. Dupont agrees to help me try to find a boat but from the look on his face I can see that he is very uncomfortable with the idea. Somehow a boat is an almost unthinkable thing.

Despite his casual demeanour, Dupont is a serious man, with a serious job. He is a journalist in a country where timely news can mean the difference between life and death. At his station, Radio Maendeleo (Radio 'Development'), he is engaged in promoting reconciliation through plays and talk shows. For journalistic purposes, he has a battered microphone, an even more battered mini-disc recorder, and three disks which he records over again and again, without archiving any of his material. He is off to visit his sister station Radio Uvira, to get an update on the local situation and he kindly takes me along.

Radio Uvira is housed in a pretty colonial building with peaked arches and whitewashed walls. Outside is a large metal aerial bowing in the wind, inside a dim warren of rooms. Several journalists are busy with recording desks and microphones and in the corner is a surprising amount of sophisticated broadcasting equipment, far more than I expected to see in a small town like Uvira. The station manager embraces Dupont and, like all educated Congolese, they greet each other in French.

The current top story is good news. The FARDC commander of the town, Colonel Mutupek, has had a car accident. It means that he is in South Africa, having treatment, and things are calmer as a result. An unruly man – a former Mai Mai warlord – he became an officer as part of the peace process and the subsequent integration of the Mai Mai militias into the official Congolese army. Overnight, with the stroke of a pen, his ragtag soldiers were transformed into the 109th Brigade. For a while he conducted his own ethnic cleansing of Uvira, rounding up all people of Banyamulenge (Congolese Tutsi) ethnicity and trucking them out of town.

'He was inciting the people against the Banyamulenge; it was getting out of hand', says the station manager.

When I was studying Swahili at the university in Dar-es-Salaam in 1996, it was derogatory slang to call someone '*banyamulenge*'; it meant trouble-maker, outsider. There were even a few buses in the city centre with *banyamulenge nuksi* (banyamulenge are trouble) emblazoned on their mud-flaps instead of the more common *mashallah* (if God wishes) or 'Jah rules' or 'love hurts'. There are nineteen thousand Congolese refugees in Burundi waiting to come home but most are Banyamulenge and they are not welcome here.

Resentment against the Banyamulenge has a long history. Eastern Congo has not escaped the struggles over land that has beset its neighbours Rwanda and Burundi. Since humans first organized themselves into groups, pressures on resources, land, grazing have easily found expression in a perceived foreign minority and the Banyamulenge outsiders fit that bill, leading some to term the Banyamulenge the 'Jews of central Africa'. It was to the Banyamulenge that Rwanda turned when it sought both allies and justification for its 1996 invasion. The rebels in wellington boots who took Kinshasa were mostly Banyamulenge, with their own reasons to resent Mobutu, who had used them as convenient scapegoats for the country's economic troubles for years. Since the break with Rwanda in 1998, and the subsequent second Congo war, the Banyamulenge have typically been seen as a dangerous fifth column, traitors to their nation. It is true that many Banyamulenge allied with the Rwandan Tutsi-led forces that committed countless atrocities in Congo and they are tainted by association; many fled to Rwanda and Burundi and no one wants them to return. And there are still flare-ups around the town of Minembwe, in the mountainous area where FARDC is pursuing the straggling Banyamulenge militias and occasionally harassing the Banyamulenge villages.

On the outskirts of Uvira is a mass of empty tents, a canvas suburb. On the roof of the largest tent is emblazoned, in enormous letters, UNHCR – United Nations High Commissioner for Refugees. When we drive past, Dupont only says a word: 'Banyamulenge'. The suburb of ghost tents that was supposed to be a place of joyful return is gradually turning from white to grey in the rain and sun.

The guys at the radio station are intrigued by my idea about seeing the aftermath of war down the lake but are sceptical about travelling by boat. They have heard of Manono – it was a strategic site during the conflict – but the only way they know how to get there is by begging the UN for a lift on one of its planes. Going overland is not even an option. People fear the spaces between the towns, where no one knows who is in charge.

Humouring me, Dupont takes me to visit a non-governmental organisation (NGO) working with returning refugees in Baraka, Kalemie and Moba, towns along the lake's shore, whose staff might know something about how to get south. Albert is the very large man in charge. His globe of a belly rests wedged behind an enormous black hardwood desk and we sit on chairs in the narrow space that remains between the desk and the wall. His jowls hang down to his collar and shake as he talks excitedly about the work of his NGO. He is delighted that someone is taking an interest in their projects; his optimism the exact opposite of Dupont's caution.

'Congo is peaceful and safe. There is no problem', he says, clapping his hands together in an act of reassurance.

Albert gives me confidence that my main problem is logistics, not insecurity or my mental health. He gives me the names of people in Baraka, the next town, about one hundred kilometres to the south. But after that, his jovial expression fades and his face goes blank.

I begin to realise that Congo is like a sea. Each of these towns is a little island community unto itself, with its own radio, market and military command. People may have news of nearby islands but beyond that, nobody knows. No one has travelled very far during the past decade of conflict, unless, perhaps, in the other direction, to Tanzania or Burundi, away from the fighting. The larger world has become strange and terrifying; people stay put and fear what they don't know. What roads exist are travelled only by aid agency workers, soldiers or adventurous business-men, and there are very few vehicles in which to move on them. At the mention of a boat, Albert's mouth turns down.

'*Ah non, c'est ça le problème*', says Albert, leaning back in his flexible office chair and repeating the word *problème* several times. Apparently, there are barges that ply the lake but none this week. One recently sank, not an uncommon event, says Albert. He looks suitably apologetic, as though Congo's limitations are a source of shame to this most hospitable man. Dupont flashes me a glum smile as if to say, 'See? Don't be an idiot'.

9

A fishless lake

Fishing on Lake Tanganyika

DUPONT IS SAD. HE may think I am crazy but like any good host he is disappointed at his inability to help me in my quest to find a boat. As consolation he takes me to eat with 'his' people, the Catholic mission. Dupont, like all educated Congolese, professes to eschew the politics of tribalism but has swapped one tribe for another. The legacy of the missionaries in the east is long but not straightforward, although wherever there are Catholics, I am coming to learn, there is always shelter and food: quite good food.

Around a gravel courtyard, under plastic awnings to protect against the fierce sun, tables and chairs form a random pattern. On two of them sit large men, adorned with gold, drinking beer. A short nun in a spotless blue habit comes to take our order.

'Fish?' I ask. Dupont smiles with the air of someone who knows the answer. The nun laughs. There is no fish. It is as though I have asked for caviar.

'But the lake is right there!' I say.

'It's complicated', replies Dupont.

There is one other customer, a thin, haggard white man with dark circles under his eyes, reading a crumpled magazine and sipping his beer in the shade of the awnings. After eating the goat stew that arrives instead of fish, I say hello. He is Alex, an aid worker with the Norwegian Refugee Council and he turns out to be precisely the man I am looking for.

'The next town along the lake is Baraka, the road there is passable in a 4x4. You can get a lift in one of my vehicles. From there you might find a boat.' Alex is generous but he doesn't humour me. 'After Baraka I don't know where you'll go or what you'll eat.'

'Surely the people in lakeside villages eat something', I ask, 'I'll offer them money and eat what they eat. Don't they fish?'

'Their old fishing nets were destroyed during the war and there's a whole host of reasons why giving them new ones is a bad idea. The UN is delivering food aid to those villages. You may find there are serious food supply issues down there', he points out professionally. 'Buy some tins. And what will you drink?'

'Whatever the people there drink', I reply.

'I wouldn't do that if I were you', he says briskly, 'Buy chlorine tablets. And what's your security strategy?'

I look at him blankly.

'You're crazy', he adds.

In the afternoon, from the way Dupont occupies himself with his tape recorder, I can tell he is in a hurry to shed my company. I leave him to his work and pay the UN a visit to see if they have any better information about what's happening further south.

The large white compound stands on the lakeshore, separated from the surf, the golden beach, the litter and the rows of dugout canoes by two lines of razor wire and a concrete wall. A very tall Senegalese man, with big hands and an expensive suit, takes me up to a first floor bar with a widescreen view of Uvira's stunning setting, its majestic mountains and sparkling lake, only slightly hampered by double-glazing and two large air-conditioning units. The Bangladeshi peacekeepers who inhabit the place are glued to the cricket on the satellite television.

Eastern Congo is a patchwork of garrisons, like those of medieval Europe, whose writ stretches only to the edge of the town and not into the hinterland beyond, and sometimes not even that far. This UN garrison has no information about what is going on outside the area they patrol; their section doesn't reach much more than a radius of about fifty kilometres. The UN missions report to the capital but not to each other. The Senegalese man can't find anyone who knows anything about the security situation even a few miles down the lake, and so he buys me a beer instead. He complains about the patrol boats that the Uvira mission had ordered but which have been pinched by the Bukavu mission, leaving the troops in Uvira with little to do.

He promises to spread the word that I am around and is true to his word. That evening two UN workers invite me to dinner in their compound. Without a nod to Uvira's hungry inhabitants, we feast on Italian food, French wine, Canadian whisky and cigars, but still no fish.

Alessandra, an ebullient Italian, thinks my plan to go south along the lake is 'wonderful'; she is jealous. On the other hand, her more austere colleague, Hunter, is full of the kinds of questions Alex had asked earlier, although being Canadian he is slightly gentler.

'I'm sorry to be alarmist but what are you going to do when a boat pulls up in front of you full of men with guns?', he asks with a frown.

I don't really know what to say. Alessandra's optimism and Hunter's caution are not based on evidence; they don't have that information. They sometimes visit the plateau above the lake by helicopter, to talk to some of the Banyamulenge rebels remaining there and try to persuade them to join the national army but apart from that they don't get out much because their movements are dictated by security protocols.

'I can't even go jogging in the hills', says Hunter.

Still, they are charming and encouraging, telling me to call if I get into any scrapes. The evening is hot and the air laced with the scent of Uvira's jacaranda trees but Hunter won't hear of me walking home and kindly drives me back to my concrete hotel.

'I hope you don't think we're too bourgeois', worries Hunter when he says goodbye, a comment to which there really is no reply.

Dupont has to go back to Bukavu and now I am the one who is depressed. He has been a delight. He has done his best to furnish me with information and contacts in the direction I want to head and that is all I can ask. He wishes me luck with a raised eyebrow, a look that I have come to fear, and as his parting shot suggests that I go and talk to the folks at the *Centre de recherches du Lac Tanganyika* who might have useful information about what's going on down the lake.

Lake Tanganyika holds mysteries that scientists still do not understand. Early European explorers came here in the nineteenth century, believing it to be the source of the Nile. In the map room at the School of Oriental and African Studies is a chart, drawn by the Roman geographer Ptolemy, of two lakes feeding the Nile, springing from the *Montes Lunae* – the Mountains of the Moon – the present-day Ruwenzoris on the Congo–Uganda border. But the Ruwenzoris are in fact several hundred miles to the north of Lake Tanganyika. A couple of Dutch maps from the 1600s show both the Nile and the Congo flowing out of a large lake north of Lake Malawi, the 'Zaire lacus'.

Europeans did not actually visit Lake Tanganyika until Burton and Speke reached Ujiji, now Kigoma, in Tanzania, in 1858, the town where Livingstone famously met Stanley thirteen years later. John Speke called the lake the 'Sea Ujiji' on the map he drew by hand in 1858 for the Royal Geographical Society, the map I saw in the SOAS library before departing on my own journey. Five years after Speke, James Augustus Grant used the Swahili name – Tanganyika – when he drafted another map for the Royal Geographic Society and the name stuck. *Tanga* means sail and *nyika* means bush, or uninhabited land. The sail in the bush: it must have been an unfamiliar sight to the Swahilis from the coast, accustomed to seeing their lateen sails in the vast blue of the ocean, not painted against rich green forest.

Early explorers continued to think the lake was the source of the Nile, but as I arrived, the bus rattled over a metal bridge that traversed a wide brown river flowing in the opposite direction, into the lake. When Livingstone and Stanley travelled here together after their famous meeting, they were bitterly disappointed to find that the Ruzizi drained into and not out of the lake. Tanganyika was not the source of the Nile.

Although that mystery was solved, others remain. Below two hundred metres, the lake's waters are without oxygen, a lifeless zone. Some scientists think it is because the water is static and that without circulation nothing can survive. But it is possible that in this volcanic region, some chemical or submerged gas (methane, carbon dioxide and sulphur dioxide are present beneath the surface) has killed off life below a certain depth.

The *Centre de recherches* is near the lake shore. Hollow-eyed people stare from shaded doorways and sleeping women slump on one arm across makeshift stalls of over-ripe fruit. Here and there are small wooden dugout canoes, pulled out of the lake and parked between low thatched huts. Beyond, the lake flashes like a sword in the afternoon heat. Despite all the canoes and drying nets slung on poles, there isn't a fish in sight.

This mystery is more pressing. The lake reputedly holds hundreds of species of fish not found anywhere else on Earth, some as yet unclassified, and Tanganyika's brightly coloured cichlids adorn aquaria the world over. But very few fish of any kind are finding their way to Uvira's market stalls or dinner plates.

The *Centre de recherches* is an enormous, imposing building with a spectacular view over the lake. Its wide façade rolls in grand steps to a wrought iron gate leading into an ageing courtyard paved with huge granite slabs. In a shallow, crumbling, tiled pool lies a motionless long-nosed crocodile. Indigenous to the lake, with its narrow barracuda-like snout and tiny teeth, it looks much more prehistoric than the familiar broken grin of the common Nile croco-dile. On one side of the courtyard, old tanks of compressed air and diving gear are covered in cobwebs, while half a motorbike slowly decomposes in an alcove. For a moment I suspect the place is abandoned but the old man sitting by the gate smiles and waves lazily to welcome me inside.

The courtyard, the fountain, the wide teak staircase, are all reminiscent of palaces built thousands of miles away, on the Indian Ocean coast, by Swahili traders, perhaps a relic of their brutal reign over this part of the Congo. The sultan of Zanzibar's envoy, the famous slave dealer Tippu Tip, was the precursor of the European brand of colonial-ism around the great lakes. I almost expect to see women in flowing black *buibuis*, the Swahili hijab, peeking out from behind the columns and the white flash of the *kanzus* of Swahili noblemen.

For nearly two hundred years, in the eighteenth and nineteenth centuries, the Zanzibaris controlled eastern Congo, from Uganda in the north to modern day Zambia in the south, building mosques, trade routes and systems of indirect rule through mini-sultans, whom the Belgians and British later called chiefs. It was the Zanzibaris with whom Burton, Speke and Stanley had to negotiate for passage and who lent them staff for their expeditions into the interior. And it was the Zanzibaris who the Belgians had to drive from the River Congo back to Lake Tanganyika to establish the Congo Free State in the name of King Leopold, eventually conquering Rwanda in 1916.

I go up the wide wooden staircase to the second floor, which looks down over the courtyard. The polished floor is solid, the paint peeling off the walls. Amid a long row of doors, one is open. Behind a desk sits a man who looks up and smiles when I tentatively rap on the giant old door. He is Gerard.

'*Approchez*, sit down, sit down', he says, while standing up himself. In this enormous building this is the only occupied office, piled high with books and reports gathering dust. Gerard is short and well-dressed, with spectacles balanced on the end of his nose; a caricature of the professor he is. Gerard is an agricultural economist, engaged in research on the state of fish stocks in the lake; it seems I might find an answer to the riddle of the missing fish of Lake Tanganyika and that I may at last be face to face with someone who has been to the villages farther along the lakeshore.

When the military occupied the centre and used it as their headquarters during the war, Gerard fled. The soldiers slept downstairs and stole the fishing equipment that he used for experiments. They used the centre's boats for transport. The academic tranquillity of the centre was shattered.

I ask him if he has ever considered getting a job abroad, going somewhere where the scientific facilities might be better.

For a moment, he gazes at me cryptically, as though he hasn't understood the question. Then he looks down and says quietly, '*Mtu kwao*'.

It is a Swahili proverb. It means 'a person belongs at home'.

His current research has been commissioned by a French NGO that, having given fishing nets to some of the returning refugees, became concerned about the effect this would have on fish stocks, suspended the programme, and called Gerard. Other charities still distribute mosquito nets, however. In the absence of the real thing, these are quickly stitched together to be used for fishing. Tragically, the holes in the nets are so fine, they catch absolutely everything. Gerard is studying the repercussions.

He is worried that the returning refugees will rapidly exhaust the fragile stocks in the lake if they are able to fish as much as they wish. Compared to eleven years ago, the last time Gerard did a survey, the number of fish being caught is going up. So far, though, several factors are keeping catches down from what it might be. Apart from the scarcity of nets, the main impediment to catching fish is the scarcity of petrol. Carved canoes, *pirogues*, cannot go too far across the lake but motor-boats can cover great distances.

'So is fish only for the rich?' I ask.

'Not at all!'

Some of the villagers catch small fry with their mosquito nets, close to the shore. Without proper nets, those with canoes can only catch single fish on a line, and without petrol cannot transport them to the big towns in good time. The ones who eat fish are mostly the fishermen, Gerard says.

'In a big town like Uvira, unless you know a fisherman, you might not taste fish for a while', he explains.

'So there are people in the villages and they have boats?' I ask somewhat nervously.

'The villages were empty until recently but people are coming back. And they have boats, yes, yes, of course.'

I ask him how one might set about travelling down the lake. He scrutinizes me hard through his steel spectacles, waits a beat, then leans back on his chair and folds his arms.

'I advise you to go to Baraka and then look for a boat. Even if you can find it, petrol is expensive, and without petrol you will have to travel in pirogues down the lake. You know, rowing, by hand. It will take a long time, many weeks. How long do you have?'

'As long as it takes'.

'Well, it might take that long', says Gerard gravely. *'Bonne chance'*.

10

The return, part I

Refugees returning to Baraka from Tanzania

THE ROAD SOUTH TO Baraka is bumpy but I am thrilled to be on it, bouncing around the cab of Alex's Norwegian relief truck as Bruno, the Congolese driver, persists in talking with his hands.

The roadside is peppered with two different kinds of hand-painted signs. The first kind is those commissioned by the community to commemorate massacres committed by the Rwandan forces and their allies during the war. Roughly drawn, lurid murals of soldiers attacking villagers sit under a banner headline of a date and massacre. The hatred against Rwanda is still strong, explains Bruno, and the local leaders are keen to keep the memories fresh.

The second kind of sign that litters every village is from the charities and international agencies who are helping the reconstruction effort. THIS TOILET WAS BUILT BY THE EUROPEAN UNION. THIS SCHOOL WAS REHABILITATED BY THE UN DEVELOPMENT PROGRAMME. Even people's houses wear little tags: A GIFT FROM DENMARK. I don't really understand why the agencies would worry about branding in a place like this, but no doubt several jobs in distant places depend on it.

The road snakes along the lakeshore, clinging to a slip of flat land at the foot of the plunging hillsides, and sometimes sheer cliffs, that crash into the lake. The forest is thick, humming with insects that rival the noise of the engine and dappled with the large flowers of frangipani and jacaranda trees in bursts of red, purple and orange. Further along, the mountains on our right recede slightly and I lose sight of the lake for the first time as the truck plunges along a sandy track choked with green. Palm trees clog the road, crowding out the taller trees behind.

It seems that we are deep in the forest, miles from anywhere but people pop out from behind trees, holding little cups overflowing with white sap in their hands. Villagers harvest pine nuts to make oil and collect the sap to make alcohol. The raw sap is already alcoholic; fermented, it becomes lethal. A group of men cooling under a tree hold out a wine bottle filled with a cloudy, milky substance and scream as we bounce past, offended that we have refused their drunken offer. 'The bush gives us everything we need', says Bruno proudly. 'We used to eat a lot of fish but now the Congolese are famous for eating anything.' Indeed, the war forced people to eat nearly every living thing: snakes, insects, monkeys, crocodiles, dogs. Bruno claims there are no crocodiles left in the lake because the soldiers shot them all. And when the villagers glimpse a hippo, they call the army to come and kill it.

'*Ça c'est la fête du village!*', cries Bruno, with a booming laugh.

There are no hotels in Baraka. It is a town dominated by NGOs dealing with the huge numbers of refugees coming back to Congo and it is at one of these that Bruno drops me off. In this post-conflict soup of humanitarian acronyms, the international agencies are the aristocracy, and, like the aristocracy, Bruno assumes both that I belong and that we all know each other.

Two French NGO workers stare at me as I emerge, dusty and sweaty, from the truck. They are Yannick and Jean-Christophe and, though they have no idea who I am, they immediately set about feeding me lunch. As far as boats south are concerned, they had one but it is broken; the only other one is owned by the UN. In any case, they say, I cannot stay with them without checking in with the authorities. So I dutifully trundle off to pay my respects to the *Directeur générale de migration*, one branch of the many-headed hydra that is Congo's government bureaucracy.

Baraka is a town bursting at the seams. At midday, the sandy streets are hot like a bath and the casual walker is soaked to the skin in about the time it would take to jump into one. The sun is blistering, yet the town is teeming with people.

The school playground brims with children, so many that they flood over the road and the churchyard. The border between the school and the road is a row of burnt-out cars. A forlorn metal sign, a souvenir from the former local petrol station, faded, colourless and riddled with bullet holes, reads FINA. Next to the school is a little wooden kiosk with a blue-painted tin roof. In big reassuring letters it is labelled BUREAU DE POLICE, BARAKA. A soldier walks past in full combat gear and wades through the children who have overflowed the playground.

Helpfully, the migration office is in the house of the officer of migration. In one room of his smoky mud hut a woman is cooking over an open fire. In the corner of another, a short bald man sits on a bench behind a small wooden table, sifting through an enormous pile of UNHCR lists of returning refugees. He wears a sharp leather jacket and very pointy black leather shoes. In the corridor several children in rags sleep on plastic bags.

Over the shoulder of the bald man, another man, tall, with greying hair and beady eyes, reads my fake letter from the University of London. The beady-eyed one also has the regulation pointy shoes, although his sport little silver tips that look as if they might do considerable damage.

They read and re-read the letter as though it contains some kind of secret information that can only be deciphered by a full five-minute stare. Maybe they cannot read French or maybe they suspect the French in my letter, since it is so badly constructed.

Since one is round and fat and the other tall and shifty, and because they appear to take their bureaucratic duties far too seriously, I nickname them Dogberry and Verges, after Shakespeare's feckless guards in *Much Ado About Nothing*. They are charming and courteous and there is no mention of money at any stage. I have no idea how much trouble they will cause.

The name Baraka is Swahili; it means 'blessing'. Maybe the slave caravans named it so, because they were so pleased to see the lake after months hacking their way through the forest. Or perhaps some early Zanzibari colonists were delighted with its temperate climate and crystal water. In any case, the town is now a blessing for the hordes travelling in the opposite direction: those who fled across the lake to Tanzania and Burundi during the war and who are now coming home. They are the living emblem of a Congo returning to peace, and I want to meet them. They are being repatriated to the isolated villages down the lakeshore and I am eager to see if I can catch a lift with the UN boat that will take them there.

The man in charge of the refugee repatriation operation, whom I must convince to grant me permission to meet the returning refugees or get a lift with them, receives me in an air-conditioned office with a miniature UN flag on the desk. The office is billeted in the second-largest building in Baraka; the largest is the church. But unlike the church, whose tall battered wooden doors are wide open, the UNHCR compound is ringed with razor wire and guarded by men with guns. The head of the office is Magatte, a tall, elegant, infinitely patient and polite man from Senegal who has been given an almost impossible job.

Ten months ago, before the repatriation operation began, Baraka was a sleepy fishing village of ten thousand people, nursing its wounds from the civil war. Now it is a bustling town of forty thousand and rising. Many of the refugees are daunted by the prospect of reclaiming their villages from the bush and rebuilding them, so they stay in the town where there is water, markets, schools and security. But Baraka cannot cope.

Magatte is at once proud of what his office has achieved but concerned at the forces that the return has unleashed. The UN charters ships that, twice a week, bring five hundred people across the lake. Even at this rate, it will take years to get everyone home. Around three million people left the country between 1996 and 2002. Half a million of those who fled ended up in camps in Tanzania and about 300,000 of them are still there, living in vast cities in the dry plains east of Lake Tanganyika. Some have been there for ten years; a generation of children brought up in refugee cities. For them, rural life will be a shock. I fear many will not survive the return to the village and will slink back to Baraka to join in the process of turning it into Congo's newest slum.

Magatte smooths his hands over the flat-pack desk and looks around his drab office as we talk, assessing his surroundings and satisfied, finding them in order, fixes his bright eyes on me again. I hesitate to ask him if I might interview the returnees. When I finally pluck up the courage, he raises his eyebrows, not in caution but in surprise. He is delighted. And he could not be more helpful. If and when there is a boat delivering refugees, I am welcome to ride on it. He has tried, unsuccessfully, to persuade several journalists to come down from North Kivu to cover this good news story, for he laments the media image of his continent as a place mainly of war, famine and AIDS.

'It is ironic, is it not', he begins in precise French, 'that while international news channels show pictures of people fleeing North Kivu, no attention at all is paid to the thousands who are returning to South Kivu'.

This, one of the largest UN repatriation exercises ever undertaken, a logistical feat of epic proportions, is almost unreported. I suppose 'People Going Home' is always going to be a less sexy headline than 'Refugees Flee Massacre'; I can also understand exactly why Magatte and his hard-working colleagues in the UN and many Congolese are piqued at the imbalance in coverage. After more than a decade of war, finally some good news! But it seems as if foreign correspondents can only see the bad; wearing the opposite of rose-tinted spectacles. Theirs are tinted a slightly darker shade: the colour of blood.

At dawn the following day I go down to the docks with Magatte to meet the newest arrivals on the incoming boat. The sky is turning gold and the water on the lake is slow and flat like hammered metal and the last of the morning mist sits heavily on the surface. A large white boat bobs gently at the quay, its deck covered in goats wearing little name tags to indicate their owner and plastic bags tied around their feet to stop them from catching foot rot from the other animals.

Through the portholes, hands poke out. The boat sounds as if it is groaning or has run aground. The mournful noise is the sound of the refugees singing in the hold; they are happy to be coming home. Since late last night their radios have been tuned to Radio Baraka.

Radio Baraka is a one-man outfit run by a determined, ageing man, Jonas, whom I had met the night before. His office is a tiny tin shack, little bigger than a toilet, with a desk and a short aerial not much taller than a tree from where he broadcasts songs of welcome across the lake to the returnees. Radio Baraka plays a key role in uniting families through its messaging service; listeners pay fifty francs to have a text message broadcast. But Jonas is more ambitious than that: he also wants bicycles for his journalists so they can report on the news farther afield, not just within Baraka. He'd like to send someone, for example, to report on the four children who were injured and the two killed at the weekend when they played with a grenade left by soldiers in a church.

On the shore, relatives have lined up behind a string and started singing. The two groups, those on the boat and those on the shore, call and answer each other like worshippers in a church. Eventually those returning come tottering down the ramp clutch identical radios, plastic flip-flops and Chinese plastic bags; they don't look well. Their eyes are red, their hair is dirty, most of the children don't have shoes and many have bloody, rotten toes. One boy's big toe is tied tightly with string to stop the rot from spreading, but the other end has burst like a sausage popped in the pan. When the crowd recognized one of their own a great cry goes up; the women ululate and clap their hands.

After taking some photos of the disembarking passengers, I board the boat to talk to some of the refugees. I am only just on deck when I notice Dogberry waving at me from where he sits on the shore, in the shade of a blue awning. I wave back but he keeps on waving. He looks agitated. I ignore him and move to go down below when a hand falls on my shoulder. I turn to see the drawn beady face of Verges looking very unhappy indeed.

'*Photo interdit*', he says, frowning and marches me off towards Dogberry and the awning.

It is, they explain, not allowed to take pictures of government property without permission. Apparently the port is government property. My argument that I have been invited by UNHCR does not wash: the boat may be UN property but the port is not.

'Most definitely not', announces Verges.

I thought they had been too kind the day before. We must, they decide, all go to the 'office', the mud hut of yesterday, to buy the necessary photography permit. There is only one problem, the port is far from the town and they don't have a vehicle so Dogberry disappears to find Magatte and beg him for a lift to return to town. When he returns, it is with a fuming Magatte in tow, who yells at the pair of them.

He has given me permission, Magatte stresses, that should suffice. They disagree but they back away all the same because to the Congolese petty officials the UN is a higher force. In a final jab they make me promise to visit the office and settle the matter later, 'otherwise there will be grave consequences'.

The humiliated officers walk away while Magatte and I catch up with the refugees in the transit camp. This is where they will spend their first night back home while they are, in Magatte's phrase, 'processed'. The process involves medical examination, rights education, food allocation and immigration bureaucracy.

In a huge tent, a dormitory, dozens of women are breastfeeding babies whilst older kids run riot across the makeshift beds and shriek through the flaps at the tent's sides. They are waiting for their turn to be examined for lice, worms and other diseases. Many of the children running around this transit camp were born in Tanzania and these are their first steps on Congolese soil.

A large truck is dispensing drinking water into plastic buckets while old men with absent eyes sit on the ground staring at the middle distance, as though they don't want to look too closely at where they are, nor focus on the green hills of home beyond: as though the story that bridges that gap is too painful to contemplate.

In another tent, an uneven line of refugees in rags shuffles from one desk to the next, accumulating forms. At the second desk I mark Dogberry and Verges, behind a tall pile of papers and an armoury of stamps, looking very important and glowering at the refugees. They see me but Verges puts his nose in the air and crosses his pointy-shoed feet before levelling his very serious gaze at a trembling old man.

Outside, eager young relief workers in red jackets and blue UN baseball caps hand out rations of food. Congo used to export forty thousand tonnes of maize a year across the lake but now the World Food Programme imports food for the returning refugees and others. At the transit camp they receive three months' supply of food per person: 36 kilos of maize flour, 10.8 kilos of beans, half a kilo of salt and 2.7 litres of cooking oil. This is what the international community has mandated it takes to keep one person alive for three months. After that, they are on their own.

Over the next few days they will be dropped, with their rations, seeds and tools, in the bush where their villages used to be. For many the challenge will prove too daunting and they will return to Baraka. After ten years in the camps in Tanzania some have forgotten how to farm, many don't want to, and most have become used to free services and food aid and to being told what to do.

'What do you expect?' says Magatte. 'There are no schools, no clinics, no functioning markets; settlement patterns will be different now.'

He is right. The problem is that no one is taking responsibility for planning Baraka's explosive transition from village to city. Once the refugees come back, the UN's job is done.

In the tent, the children crowd around, hanging on each other's shoulders, disappearing as soon as I direct a question at any one in particular. They are polite, shy and unfailingly optimistic and they speak grammatically correct Tanzanian Swahili; a product of the camps. I ask them what they are looking forward to, coming home.

Every single child wants to go to school. Nothing else. No talk of clothes, or food, or money. In the Tanzanian camps the schools were free. It breaks my heart to hear their hopes; Congo does not have enough schools even for those who are already here. Brought up in the relative entitlement of the refugee camps, where everything was laid on, I suspect they will find freedom in their homeland more than a little disappointing.

The women want land, their only real safety net, to grow their own food. One old woman is not sure if her plot will still be there when she gets back.

'What will you do if someone else has stolen it?' I ask her.

'I'll buy another one.'

'With what money?'

'I'll sell my food rations.'

'And then how will you eat?'

'I might be hungry for a while but then I know that next year and the year after that, I'll be able to eat.'

It will be hard, but she is ready for the struggle.

'Would you rather have stayed in the refugee camp?' I ask.

'NO', comes the chorus from her and from all the other women listening to our conversation.

'This is our home. This is our land. This is where God means us to be', says a large woman in a brightly coloured head wrap. She has learned English in the refugee camps and earned money making clothes which she now intends to use to open a school back in Congo. It will be a good business.

There is one old man in the tent, sitting on a mattress with his walking stick between his legs. He beckons me over and asks what I am doing. Whatever it is I am handing out, he wants some of it.

'I'm asking people what they hope to do now they are home, after the war', I say.

'I have nothing to say. I have already achieved my wish', he says.

'What was that?'

He fled Congo twice. He rebuilt his home twice. This is the third time he has returned across the lake; he sneaked back last year to register and vote in the elections but then had to go back and collect his family from Tanzania.

'I am Congolese. If there is an election I must vote, I must be heard. Is it not so?' he says proudly. 'That was my wish, to vote.'

Magatte comes in and gives a short speech in French exhorting them not to sell their food rations. I catch the eye of the old woman and she winks at me. They may be poor but these people are in control of their destiny once more. This is what dignity means, to be able to decide how your own meagre resources are used. Queuing for food, for shelter, waiting for someone else to decide your circumstances is a kind of humiliation. No matter that the provisions in the refugee camps were free. The returnees are not only regaining their country, but their autonomy, their selfhood, too.

That's not quite how those that didn't flee see things. The repatriation process has created a new social cleavage in Baraka: those with new machetes, blue UNHCR buckets and reserves of food tucked away, and those without. Baraka is buzzing because of the money being spent on returning refugees but these services are temporary. When the NGOs go home, the Congolese government will be in no position to pick up the pieces. The free clinics will turn into fee-paying ones, the food and water hand-outs will stop. At that point the returnees will face the full experience of surviving in post-war Congo. The privileged refugees with their rations, seeds and tools will experience what it was like for the millions who could not find the fifteen dollars it took to flee across the lake to Tanzania, or who ran in the wrong direction.

These are the people about whom Roelant, from *Médecins Sans Frontières*, is concerned. Roelant is one of the small number of dedicated foreigners working in Baraka who are trying to get their agencies to pay more attention to the Congolese who didn't cross an international border and earn themselves the title 'refugee'. As the agencies gear up to leave, Roelant thinks they should stay but focus elsewhere. He is a huge, brawny, blond Dutchman who says the best preparation for working in Congo was his formative career smuggling jeans into Soviet Russia.

'The returnees are fine. They're getting lots of help', he says, 'but the Banyamulenge, they're not getting any'.

No one, certainly not the Congolese government, it seems, is too worried about the welfare of the Banyamulenge. They are hard to reach: no roads climb up into the cool green mountains above Baraka where they live. Roelant has set up one small clinic, a day's walk into the hills above the town but no other agencies are working up there and even he hasn't been to visit the clinic for many months, because running the hospital in Baraka keeps him busy. But, a true activist, Roelant is passionate about the needs of the people the agencies are not reaching and he wants me to go and visit his clinic up in the mountains.

I am keen to hear their side of the story, to hear what they think about their compatriots who seem to hate them with an irrational passion. The Banyamulenge have played a key part in recent Congolese history and if war comes again, they will be on the front line once more. While peace seems to be holding elsewhere, the Mulenge plateau is restive. Citing fears about the 'Balkanization' of Congo, ethnic Bemba and Bafuliro politicians from Uvira are campaigning for the Banyamulenge territory of Minembwe to be subsumed within neighbouring Fizi (where Baraka belongs). While Banyamulenge militias, unconvinced of the government's plans for their people, are refusing to disarm.

I have time to explore this tangled story of mistrust. It will be several days before there is a possibility of any boat leaving Baraka, since the French NGO boat is still broken and Magatte is not sure when the next UN one will go; maybe next week. After the cloying heat and bursting streets, some mountain air will be no bad thing.

I am not keen, however, to hand over more of my precious francs to the insatiable Congolese bureaucracy, so I don't go and see Dogberry and Verges as I promised. They send messages to the French NGO, summoning me to the official hut, but I hide. Instead, Yannick calls the head office to see if he can smooth things over. Amazingly, Dogberry and Verges' commander is patently unapologetic. The slim opportunities for extortion from foreigners must be seized upon, he says, and everyone must get their cut; it is a question of fairness. In the end I skip town and run for the Mulenge hills, which, I suppose, technically makes me a fugitive.

11

Trouble in the Mulenge hills

The Mulenge hills, nearly cleared of all trees

REACHING THE MOUNTAIN HOME of the Banyamulenge is hard. There is much more contact across and along the lake than with the mountains that overshadow it. There is one road to Minembwe, the capital of the territory but to get there one must drive around to the plateau from the lakeshore. The rest of the hills are accessible only on foot; they remain a kind of highland fortress, keeping watch over Congo's eastern frontier.

The *Médecins Sans Frontières* clinic is at a place called Bibokoboko in the lower mountains, the *moyenne*, as they are called. It's a full day's steep climb to reach it but fitness is not the only challenge: the mountains are also technically a war zone.

In a minor conflict not deemed worthy of international attention, the newly formed Congolese army is fighting Banyamulenge guerrillas who have refused to integrate their forces with it. The *Forces armées de la République Démocratique du Congo* is a huge unwieldy being, a menacing presence without a head that is slowly growing as, one by one, the armed groups that ravaged the country join it. The Mai Mai militias that are enlisting simply don FARDC uniforms as protection. The Banyamulenge, however, are refusing; they don't trust their would-be comrades-in-arms.

These hundreds of thousands of armed men haphazardly, but effectively, control Congo. They are quasi-feudal rulers where there is no rule of law, and people are scared of them. Mostly, the community puts up with military occupation as a random, unpredictable force in their lives, like the weather. But army permission is required to enter the militarized zone and its leader here in Baraka is Major Davide.

It is amazing, given that Baraka is littered with soldiers lounging over vehicles along the main street, smoking or begging for cigarettes, drinking in bars, wandering through school grounds, that their leader is nowhere to be found. At the barracks a young and confused soldier sends me to the *état major*. There, they send me back to the barracks. I give up.

Often, the best way to solve a difficult problem in Congo is to get drunk, and what's more it's my birthday, so it seems like the perfect idea. It so happens that Baraka's only nightclub, Club VIP, the hottest joint for hundreds of miles, is having an opening party tonight. On the door is a hand-drawn paper bearing a picture of a man in a vest, a picture of a foot wearing a sandal and a picture of a gun. Each picture has a red cross drawn over it: 'no vests, no sandals, no machine guns'. In that order. Priorities in Congo are different.

My new friend Roelant from *Médecins Sans Frontières* spots me and calls me over to his table. Spreading his huge arms wide, over the deafening music he shouts in his big Dutch–French voice, 'Ben! You must meet Major Davide. He is the commander of the …'

'I know.'

Of course, to find the elite, and that's what the military are, I should have immediately gone to the most expensive bar in town. Major Davide is short and round. He has thick glasses that give him an unseeing gaze, except when he looks straight at you. Then, his eyes loom large, swallowing his face; they are wet, as are his lips. He drinks his beer slowly, like a baked, bug-eyed frog feasting slowly on all the females in the place. It is clearly not the first beer of the day.

He says little and is uninterested in my plan to visit Bibokoboko. He is far more concerned that I appreciate his Belgian citizenship, gained through a previous relationship with a Belgian woman.

'You see me here, but you do not see me. I am Belgian', he says, slamming his beer glass on the tin table for emphasis.

Davide is a soldier I would not like to meet sober. If this is the sort of man in whose hands Congo's governance rests, the country has a long way to go. But in a bar, on my birthday, he is a harmless spectacle. Perhaps his permission is irrelevant anyway. I will go to the mountains and meet soldiers who probably don't even know who the commander in Baraka is, and they will rob or shoot me as their fancy takes them.

There is no road to Bibokoboko, only a path. The Mulenge hills climb sharply from the shore of the lake to over three thousand metres, in two steps. The *moyenne* plateau is the first step and the *haute* plateau the higher, second one. The feet of the hills dip their toes in the lake and bathe in the heat while the peaks cool in the luxuriant mist and clouds.

The path begins amid the gardens of the lakeside Bemba people. Bamboo, sugar cane, and maize spring from the thick red soil with enthusiasm. It's just after dawn but the fields are already alive with people chopping, hoeing, gathering, pulling life from the earth.

Once upon a time, these hills were populated by hunter-gatherers, the Batwa (otherwise known as pygmies), while the foothills were tilled by the majority local tribe, the Bemba. The Bemba name for the hills, Mulenge, is used now. In the nineteenth century, however, Tutsi herders fleeing the tyrannical king of Rwanda, Rwabugiri

(1853–97), travelled south with their cattle, heading for the fertile grazing of these highlands that bordered Lake Tanganyika. In a bid to enhance their legitimacy as Congolese natives, the Tutsis took to calling themselves Banyamulenge, literally 'the people of the Mulenge hills'. Over time, the Banyamulenge colonized the hills with their cattle and the Bemba were pushed lower down the mountains. The Belgians made things worse, encouraging more Rwandans to migrate to Congo to relieve overcrowding.

Claude, my reluctant guide, insisted on by Roelant, is a nurse from the hospital. As the path gets steeper he lights a cigarette.

'It wakes up the lungs', he says, with a throaty laugh.

At first the path is alternately white and red, studded here and there with granite slabs and shards of a green rock, then a dazzling white paved with sheets of quartz. We take a break at the top of the next hill, beside the shell of a church. Looking back, morning has broken in spectacular fashion all along the lake's shore. From here, the canoes resemble specks of iron filings floating on the water's surface. The lake is deep and the light refracted up from the depths is a rich royal blue. We are only a few hundred metres above Baraka but already the air is cooler and the branches are thronged with birds, lined up as if in church: starlings, lilac-breasted rollers, bee-eaters and finches hymn, chatter and gossip, appraising us, the new visitors.

The beauty of the setting offsets the tragedy written on the hillside. The altar of the old church crumbles and tiles from the roof lie smashed and scattered across the baked mud floor. Surrounding it are the overgrown foundations of razed huts but the adjacent fields are being cleared. Where once the Banyamulenge's enemies burnt their crops and villages, they now covet their land and cultivate it. The chatter of the birds abates for a moment as a voice calls out. 'Claude! How are you doing?' From nowhere an old friend of Claude's appears on the path up the mountain.

They are from the same town, Bukavu, the capital of South Kivu province, hundreds of miles away. It turns out they haven't seen each other for five years. Paul says he has come here to 'find life', as the saying goes in Swahili. Bukavu was too crowded and here, he has found, there is plenty of land, even if it does officially belong to someone else. In the post-war period, people are ranging far in search of 'life' and using any means necessary to secure it. Plots are measured here in terms of grazing; one with enough grazing for two cows costs ten dollars if you buy it legally. Paul thinks that's too much.

'It's better to simply take. There have been some fights. One man from Bukavu that I know fought with a Banyamulenge but the Banyamulenge beat him with the law.' A rare legal victory I suspect.

Paul justifies his stealing by claiming that the Banyamulenge are not Congolese but Rwandan. Prejudice, however, can be overcome by other needs.

'So, how's life, are you married?' asks Claude.

'Well, there was this one Banyamulenge woman, she needed help with her plot but you know how they are ...'

Claude nods his head knowingly.

We leave Paul to contemplate his loneliness and his plot of land. Around the next corner is a stream where a woman and her children are washing clothes. They put down the washing and come and shake our hands one by one, even the small girls, looking directly at us with their large, otherworldly, Tutsi eyes. The excessive formality is a bit disconcerting, but it is their way, and it is a beautiful gesture.

'They are not all bad', says Claude, for the world has just contradicted him, 'and they are very polite'.

At Bibokoboko, the rounded hills run away into the blue horizon. In the purpling sky, all manner of birds sing and squawk in the branches of the huge trees that march along the ridge. A pair of hornbills swoop low over the path from the river and disappear into the canopy, whilst below the way is lined with violets and wild orchids. On a grassy lawn running up the final hill cows graze lazily, fat and glossy, like a Swiss postcard.

On the top of the hill is a collection of round huts, painted pink. To one side, facing the setting sun, is a large church built of mud and roofed with corrugated iron, while just below is a small concrete building, overlooking a ravine; the health centre. After eight hours on our feet, never before has such a rough and simple building looked so lovely. Claude allows himself his first drink of water of the day; I, on the other hand, collapse.

I'm completely exhausted. It has been a very stiff walk, like climbing stairs for a whole day, but formalities must be observed, and I am dragged off to meet the most senior man in the village, the pastor. He writes his name in curly script in my notebook: Rusamontereko Byabagabo.

Rusamontereko is a kind man with a quiet voice. He can see my legs are shaking and he promises to keep things brief. But by the time he has finished, there are twenty men in the church, eager to know my business. It has been a long time since anyone came to the hills and asked the Banyamulenge how they feel about anything. They are angry about the Bemba's hatred; they call them 'the people of the lake'. And angry about the current military operation, a result, they say, of discrimination by the government and the UN.

'We are named after these hills. They are ours. Our neighbours are jealous of our cattle. Our neighbours say that we are not Congomen, because we do not mix with them. Our faces are different, as you can see', says one old man with a stick as tall as himself.

It is true; the tall Tutsis stand out, with their high foreheads, defined cheekbones and large dreamy eyes, a bit like those of their beloved cattle.

'The army behaves as though we are the enemy, in our own land!'

Heads nod vigorously all around the church. A young man, François, is bolder than the rest, 'The rebels, the Gumino, they are right!' he shouts.

Gumino means 'we stay here' in the Banyamulenge language. Apparently the rebels are afraid of integrating into the FARDC because the last time they participated in the national army, in 1998, the Banyamulenge units were massacred by their comrades. This is the source of their distrust. Passions run high and the air is thick with tension.

The pastor valiantly tries to cool things. 'We want peace. But above all what we want is a road. Go and tell your people to build us a road, then NGOs can come and bring us assistance', he says.

Roads in eastern Congo can be a mixed blessing. The roads the Belgians built were laid with slave labour and were used for transporting goods out of the country, not for bringing services in. A road built by a French charity up to Minembwe, on the *haute* plateau, was closely followed by an upsurge in military operations, as the army could then move men and munitions more easily, so a road built to improve humanitarian access has instead brought war into the hills and ferries the inhabitants out as they flee the conflict. I wonder whether the pastor perhaps does not know or appreciate these facts.

The remoteness of my hosts may afford them greater security from the army but it is not for me to tell them that. All I can do is nod and smile at the long row of drawn, weathered faces poking out of frayed suit jackets and from beneath battered felt hats and agree to take their message to 'my people', whoever they may be. As the daylight drains from the church, I pass along the row of village elders and clasp each outstretched hand, one by one. I am shocked by their size and texture. The rough, leathery palms are cold as rocks; their hands have taken on the features of their beloved landscape and speak more than do their words of a lifetime of dedication to this land. Whatever others may say about them, these men must indeed know these hills like their own skin.

12

The end is nigh

A traditional Banyamulenge village

EARLY THE NEXT MORNING, Simba wakes me from what would probably be an eternal slumber in a wooden cot in the two-bed 'ward' of the health centre. Simba is the grumpy but efficient nurse at the centre and he is my host. His name means 'lion' in Swahili and he does indeed have a face a bit like a cat. He moves, however, like a hippo, with a lumbering gait.

I have one day in the mountain kingdom of the Banyamulenge before I must return to the lakeshore. Simba has agreed to lead Claude and me to the next large village, Magunga; a three-hour walk.

'Of course, if you weren't here, it would only be one and half', says Simba, with the first shade of a smile he's shown all morning.

The Banyamulenge are very good at walking. The path from Baraka, which rises one thousand metres, took me eight hours to climb. Simba laughs at me.

'I can go down and up again in five!'

It is Sunday and Simba is dressed in his best outfit: patent leather shoes, pressed trousers, a red shirt and a grey jacket. Despite the dusty path his shoes shine throughout the day.

The air is sweet up here; breathing is easier. Magunga is further out on the *moyenne* plateau, nearer the fighting. The hills stretch out, recalling the downland of southern England. Knobbly knuckles of hills hold mauve shadows in their joints, their tops brushed white with mist. Looking down into the valleys, the trees are the bright hue of a lawn after rain while the grass and scrub on the top of the hills is yellow, red and black, where the bush has been burned.

It is the end of the dry season and the bush has been cleared for planting. The rains are coming soon. On every mountainside black squares turn brown with digging and then green with the planting of cassava cuttings. You can tell how busy a farmer has been by the colour of his plot. And all along the horizon the blue wall of the *haute* plateau rises to double the altitude of the *moyenne*, the rim of a bowl dropped from heaven.

These hills are a militarized zone; there is an ever-present risk of government checkpoints and patrols. Claude is from the Barega tribe, near Bukavu, an innocuous identity in Congo, while Simba is a Banyamulenge from near the village where we are headed, a native. Walking with them both means I have two passports in this fractured land.

The path follows the folds of the hills before descending into a knuckle amid thick forest to arrive at a wide, brown, fast-flowing river, its banks streaked with orange silt. Several stepping-stones lead to a twisted branch that shivers underfoot. Rising on the other side I find the reason for the silt: cut into the riverbank are broad trenches of deep red mud and orange quartz stones. It is a gold mine. But no one is there today.

'Why?' I ask Simba.

'It is the day of God, Sunday', he replies without a smile, as if I am both a heretic and a fool.

A group of little girls trips along the path carrying cassava tied in bunches with coloured cloth, gifts for the people they are going to visit in neighbouring villages. Several old men in felt hats, wearing suit jackets over ragged trousers and clutching worn sticks in their worn hands, finger their lapels and extend their heavy worn hands as we pass. '*Bonjour!*' they shout in loud voices.

We must greet everyone on the road because, in this tightly knit rural community, it is the Banyamulenge way of doing things. They expect to know who I am, where I am going and what I am doing in their hills. So to each, Simba must explain. It takes time but I like this formal custom; it assumes that everyone is equal and has a right to know. If I were bringing money or development projects, they would follow it up with their leaders; a cultural system of accountability in a country that has otherwise forgotten the meaning of the word.

Three boys driving cows let their animals wander amid the scrub and walk over to offer their hands. One carries a machete, one a stick and one an umbrella. None have shoes. Simba tells them our mission and they extend their hands once more, bowing slightly, faces grave.

'Welcome', says one in English, extremely pleased and allowing himself a little grin.

We go up, then down, through forest, then burnt grass, more times than I can count. Eventually, we drop down through sloping trees to another river, wider than the last. The gold mining here has left long strings of quartz deposits that glint in the riverbed. The rush of a waterfall is punctuated by the chop, chop of a shovel somewhere among the trees.

'Bamushi ... godless people', mutters Simba. The Bamushi are the traditional miners in Congo. They come from the area around Bukavu, where gold was first found, and so mining has become 'their' vocation more than other tribes. The Banyamulenge do not mine their hills. I ask Simba why.

'It is not our calling. God wanted us to be herders, and He gave us cattle.' It is as simple as that. Never mind that the mine yields much more riches than a cow. These proud Banyamulenge seem to have another agenda, a deep attachment to a proven way of life which they are reluctant to endanger.

The path up to Magunga seems to climb into the sky. This town, too, is built on a hilltop surrounded by grassy slopes that fall away to wooded valleys bursting with foliage and birdsong, but as we gain the summit and stroll into town, it is silent. The narrow muddy streets wind their way between deserted mud huts painted blue, green, and yellow. The mud of the streets is churned with signs of a recent stampede, hundreds of bare human feet, as though a plague or an army has torn through the town moments before. It is Sunday, and in this devout place mass has emptied the streets.

A stray young man in a purple suit and shiny brown shoes greets and escorts us to a church, packed to the rafters. People are pushing at the back to get a better view. A tall pastor in a navy tailored suit jumps up and down, shouting 'Jesu Christu! Jesu Christu!' The altar is a wooden table with an elaborate tablecloth. The floor is mud, the roof tin. The pastor stops his preaching, bends to wipe his brow with a handkerchief and welcomes us in French and Swahili before resuming his sermon in three local languages: Swahili, Kibembe, and Kinyamulenge; evidence of Magunga's cosmopolitan nature, partly because of the mines.

A choir begins singing, beautifully, effortlessly, accompanied by a traditional drum. It is arresting, haunting, and for a moment I am transported by the rich harmony that seems to envelop the hundreds who have gathered in this small tin-roofed church; it carries us on a wave towards a promised land. Then, with a crash, the moment is destroyed by the entrance of an electric piano whose programmed beats are powered by a car battery.

Outside the church, past a now familiar line of old men shaking hands and tipping felt hats, Claude introduces me to a man whose brown three-piece suit is less frayed than those of the others. He is Lawi, the *Chef de section*, the nominal representative of the Congolese government in the village. We follow *Chef* Lawi into one of the larger tin-roofed homes and through to a dining room with a dark table, wooden dresser and upholstered, three-piece suite. But for the twenty elders with muddy feet, ragged suits and milky eyes who crowd in after us and sit on the floor, we could be in a rural Belgian farmhouse.

Lawi expresses the collective position of the community on their history and their right to inhabit the Mulenge hills. The others are there to make sure that he tells the story right. And they will be sure to correct him when he gets it wrong. All eyes are on him as he speaks and the crowd murmurs, shuffles and sways to his words.

'We were here before the Belgians, we were here before the Germans, even before the Swahili Arabs. When they came they just sold people down at the lake and went on their way, they did not come into our hills. When we came here there was nothing, it was wild.' To prove the point Lawi asks one old man to stand up.

'His elder brother was eaten by a lion in 1924!'

I ask how life was under the Belgians and everyone looks at the man, who is still standing, holding on to the shoulder of a younger man for support. He speaks slowly and gesticulates at another old man in a felt hat and dark suit, to his left. Many years before, the two men had carried a Belgian on a sedan chair, when he came to count the cows.

'The Belgian was a veterinary, a doctor of cows.'

The two men carried the vet for four days. The skin on their shoulders came off and when they stopped they were beaten. If the chair fell, they were beaten on the head.

The job may have only been for four days but it took them months to recover. The crowd murmurs assent.

'I still have the scars on my back', says the old porter.

We talk for several hours until a large pot of chicken stew arrives. Since the army came, chicken has become a delicacy. There is a military post just below Magunga village and the elders are not happy about it. The soldiers stop people on the road and steal their livestock and crops. They are parasites on the community, not icons of law, order and security. The elders claim the military build their positions near villages so that the Gumino rebels will be afraid to attack.

'We are like a human shield', says one.

Afterwards, the convocation of old men walks us to the edge of their hill. Lawi, topped with a felt hat, gripping a shortwave radio held together with tape, leads the way. The Banyamulenge have no radio station up here. They listen avidly to *Radio France* and BBC French and Swahili but they are angry about the coverage, which they feel doesn't do them justice: it is a one-sided conversation. No one visits them, no one hears their side of the story. This is exactly why I came. They insist on recording a long interview in Swahili stating their view of things, the view from the Mulenge hills, which I must take to the BBC in London, so that their words can be heard.

As we take our leave and descend the hill, the pastor loudly warns anyone who will listen that the war in the mountains is a sign of the beginning of the end; the apocalypse of the Book of Revelation. Lawi and the others nod their heads. This is an article of faith among many in eastern Congo. How else can one explain such unremitting destruction?

On the journey home, I ask Simba and Claude whether they agree.

'Pastors are just politicians', says Simba, 'they cheat people just the same. They always say 'the end is coming, the end is coming' but it never does. And still they want money. What do they want money for if the end is coming?'

'Do you go to church? Do you give money?' I ask him.

'Yes, of course, I'm Pentecostal', replies Simba, as if there is no relationship between his opinions and his actions.

The evangelical churches have established themselves like an alien weed in the culture of the Banyamulenge. They have become part of the structure of tradition and authority. To reject the church is to reject the community and so one must attend, pray and give tithes, in almost medieval fashion. Claude and Simba might deride the church in private but come Sunday, they will be in the front row.

We make slow progress through the afternoon, shaking hands all along the path. In a glade flecked with yellow flowers, behind a tree with brilliant red leaves that has been felled across the path, I notice three young grinning faces. The children, between five and eight years old, have smashed a termite mound and cut the tree to extract sap. They smear the glue of the sap on a branch and stick termites on. Birds that come to eat the termites will get stuck, too and will, in their turn, have their songs silenced by these smiling little predators.

Walking up the other side of the valley, we pass steep gullies that have been washed out of the hillside by the rain. The unearthed quartz sparkles in the afternoon light. The trees are enormous, a vestige of the mighty forest that must once have stretched all the way to the Atlantic Ocean; its eastern fringe is receding from the lake and towards the sea at an unhealthy rapid rate. These massive survivors must be hundreds of years old. They stand on the ridge like a glowering reproach; they are the price for the tidy complacency of the Banyamulenge's patchwork of fields and the Tutsi cattle of the Mulenge hills. Two grey parrots squawk in agreement and take to the air, circling in the lavender dusk.

It is night when we get back to Bibokoboko. There are no lights in the hills, only the glow of fires set to clear the bush. When I wake at four, I discover that a woman has just given birth to a girl, the first of twins. Nwajor, a nurse at the clinic, has been up all night helping through the long labour but I heard nothing: the mother made no sound. Nwajor bids me farewell and tells me that if the second child is a boy, the mother has promised to name him after me, in honour of the stranger who came to the hills to visit her people. I would love to stay but it is too risky to tarry in the hills and besides, I have an appointment with a boat in Baraka. At least, I hope so.

In the pre-dawn morning, two lonely stars and a half moon guide us back down to the lake. As we descend to the misty lakeshore, a slim peninsula of land takes shape slowly, dark against the waters, a giant crocodile's head dozing in the shallows. It is a glimpse of the way south; from up here, my goal, for the first time, doesn't seem impossible.

When I look back at the hills that will shadow me south, I will remember fondly the gentleness and resilience of these persecuted mountain people. The strength of Banyamulenge traditions belie their idea that the apocalypse is coming. Like the Jews of Europe, these people will work all the harder to sustain their ways because they feel the responsibility and the discipline of the victim. I am impressed by their pride in the face of persecution and, in a moment of hope as well as vanity, I imagine a man called Ben, with heavy furrowed hands and a felt hat, walking the Mulenge hills eighty years from now.

13

In search of goats and gold

Bwalile aboard the *Nyota ya Bahari*, Kazimiya

WHEN I RETURN TO the swelter of Baraka, hot, sweaty and with aching legs, Yannick is standing in the courtyard of the NGO, pulling on a cigarette. He catches sight of me and breaks into a broad grin.

'What are you laughing at?' I demand to know.

'There's good news for you', he says.

'What?'

'We're sending some people to check on our goats. In a boat. Going south. You can catch a ride.'

Yannick's charity gives out seeds and tools to the returnees; they also organize self-help groups to start commercial projects, like opening a village bakery or tailor or breeding goats. In the goat-breeding programme, a group of six people take delivery of a female goat, impregnate it by one of the other goats in the village and distribute the offspring within the group. The process repeats until everyone in the group has their own goat from which to begin breeding their own flock. Since so much livestock disappeared during the war, and since goats are a key source of milk as well as meat, it appears to be a very sensible idea.

The French NGO has hired a boat to deliver a shipment of sewing machines and check up on the goats that they delivered last time. It leaves tomorrow and I am welcome to hitch a lift. It will turn around, somewhere around Yungu or Talama, and come back again after a week, reports Yannick. These places feel very far away: I have become Congolese in my mental geography and next week is impossible to imagine. I don't know if I'll ever get that far south, or indeed to Manono, but at least the first part of my plan is coming together.

At the appointed time the following morning, I go down to the beach at Baraka to wait for the boat. Stanley, on reaching this part of the lakeshore in 1895, said of the inhabitants: 'the fishermen evidently think themselves comfortably situated … nature has supplied them bountifully with all that a man's heart or stomach can desire'. Times have changed.

Today, everyone in Congo is struggling to eat; the usual approach is to use all means at your disposal, to steal, extort or simply beg for whatever bounty that passes by. A position of authority is, of course, the best vantage point from which to glean at least a meagre harvest, and ports and roadblocks are a favoured habitat among government officials who can easily cream off a percentage of the trade that is beginning to trickle in with the peace. Even our mercy mission must bribe its way out of port.

The state has grown like the water hyacinth that clogs the Congo River, making the system impossible to navigate. Petty officials choke every transaction or movement of goods and people. Soon the state will choke itself.

Mashine, the captain of our ship, comes into view, surrounded by a cacophonous crowd of representatives from different branches of the hyacinth bureaucracy, who are waving, variously, an AK-47, pieces of paper, some kind of official stamp and a camera. One of the many officious, nondescript men in bad suits demands that Mashine purchase a driving licence (to allow him to carry foreign passengers). A soldier with a gun is demanding an embarkation fee (for protecting us from pirates, even though we are on land).

Most ingenious of all is the man with the camera. He is in military uniform but, instead of a gun, he brandishes his camera, which he waves at the officials while instructing them not to bother us. When we board the boat, he demands his reward for 'protecting' us from the 'corrupt and godless Congolese government'. Mashine laughs at him and starts the motor. As we move away from the beach, in the most comical threat I have encountered so far, the cameraman presses the shutter violently several times, as though it were a gun. There is nowhere to buy film for hundreds of miles.

We are off and soon the only sound is the quiet sawing of the engine and surf stroking the side of the boat. It is a handsome motorboat, about thirty feet long, with no roof or deck, just some planking around the edge, like a window sill, on which we sit, sleep and eat. In wide white letters painted in an arc above the bow is the name – *Nyota ya Bahari* (Star of the Sea).

Lake Tanganyika, almost a sea, is a luxurious aquamarine, mirroring the hot, flat sky. On our right-hand side, the wooded shore of Ubwari keeps pace with our ship, like a constant friend. Its thick tangled magnificence is a deep mysterious sage-green; I imagine other-worldly creatures stalking below the canopy, the life of the forest untroubled by Congo's waves of conquerors. There are some places man can never rule. The colour is murky and mesmerizing and I find myself staring at it for hours, imagining Manono somewhere on the other side. At points when, almost beyond our will, we are drawn in close to the forest, I fear a liana will whip out and seize me, or a snake with a mind of its own will grab one of us to feast on. When we are farther out, the vegetation just a slash, a third of the horizon rather than the hungry, humming abyss that filled the sky, I breathe more easily. The thought of a mile of water below, populated by unknown prehistoric monsters, is somehow less terrifying.

The crew are pleased to be under way. As I will come to learn, when they are happy and content, they make fun of each other incessantly. They are ridiculous and wonderful in equal measure, a Laurel and Hardy routine, except there are three of them.

Mashine swears that his mother named him deliberately, so that he should end up working with machines, his job with boat engines conveniently being evidence of his mother's prophetic powers. So convinced is he of the utter incompetence of his fellow crew members that even a simple glance at them is often enough to spark a burst of giggles from the enormous mouth that frames his enormous teeth. Most of the time, Mashine holds the tiller with a professional air. On the occasions when he doesn't, he either leaps about the boat like Spiderman or sits astride the bow, staring out at the blue lake as if glued to some secret television drama, every so often turning his head and flashing grins at the rest of the boat.

Gilet is, to give Mashine his due, often stupidly incompetent. But he is the one who knows the lake the best, having ferried weapons from Tanzania, and refugees in the opposite direction, during the war. Many of these journeys were made at night and he knows its inlets and promontories like the limbs of a lover. Gilet is large and powerful but his voice has the high-pitched squeak of a chihuahua. He acquired his name because he is obsessive about wearing an orange life jacket. Perhaps experience has taught him its value. Mashine refuses completely to wear one – it is unnecessary, he explains, for he is a man of the water; yet, strangely, Gilet is the only one of the three who can swim.

Bwalile is the quietest of the group. He moves slowly and deliberately around the boat, wary of the water that he cannot swim in. He spends the majority of the voyage at the bottom of the hold, bailing water, a position from which the other two derive immense enjoyment. 'Look at him, he's still there!' cry Mashine and Gilet every time Bwalile goes down beneath the gunwales, which is often. They roll around on deck, doubled up.

It is a surprise when, a week later, I discover that Bwalile, and not Mashine, is the captain of the boat. Once the truth is known, Mashine and Gilet push him around and laugh all the more.

'Hah-hah, "Captain", you are doing the menial job of bailing again, hah, hah, what kind of captain are you!?'

Bwalile smiles his crooked enigmatic half-smile, widens his eyes and returns to his task. During the war, Bwalile was assistant to Dunya, the feared Mai Mai general, a native of Ubwari, whose forces still control all the territory hereabouts. Dunya is also the owner of our boat, another source of much hilarity to the crew. As always in Congo, the economy is entwined with the conflict and so this boat taking goodwill supplies to the refugees is also providing profit to a man who caused many of them to flee in the first place. Yet the French charity has few alternatives. There are few boats left intact after the war, so doing business with the warlord is their only, reluctant, option.

Yvette and Bienvenue are the other two members of our merry band and the only proper paying passengers. The sun is intense, the cobalt water is staggering but they are not admiring the view. They stare at the water rushing past the hull, contemplating their misfortune. They are town people, professionals, and going to the village – or, as they call it, 'the bush' – is seen as punishment. The United Nations High Commissioner for Refugees has subcontracted the work of helping the repatriated to the French

NGO and it, in turn, has hired Yvette and Bienvenue. These two unlikely characters are the international community's representatives in its effort to assist the Congolese after a decade of war; the front line of international aid and donations, a fact that makes me chuckle.

In a land where jobs are gold dust, Yvette and Bienvenue are at the top of the pecking order and they waste no opportunity to remind the others of it. When the crew buy fish from a passing canoe, Yvette stands over Bwalile telling him how to grill it, then offers the finished product to me before flaking a little on to a plate for the crew and promptly finishing off the rest herself. She may work for a charity but her attachment to her class won't allow her to exercise any charity herself.

Bienvenue is less fierce; the very opposite. He has a curious expression stuck on his face, as if he is permanently on the verge of tears. Impeccably dressed, he puts on a new matching outfit every day. Today, his checked shorts and spats give him the air of a golfer. Perched on the prow, he looks as though he might at any moment call 'Fore!' and launch a drive into the blue horizon.

Our route takes us all the way around the Ubwari peninsula, a long finger of land that juts out into Tanganyika, shielding Baraka from the fierce storms of the lake. During the war, Ubwari was occupied by Rwandans, then Burundians, then by Dunya's gang. The peninsula emptied as villagers fled to Tanzania on any craft that would take them. Now, twice a week, the UN is bringing them home.

The first village we visit is on the very tip of the peninsula, pointing northeast. It is twin villages: Mizimu and Dine. We pull up on a beach that could be in a tourist video, as transparent water laps against golden sand fringed with large granite boulders. Mizimu itself is like a film set. It buzzes with activity; in every direction, post-conflict projects are well underway: a new school, a new clinic, houses. We find the chief holding a megaphone on the site of the new clinic. He wears ripped jeans, a military shirt and a strange black hat, a bit like a Moravian peasant. He has been chief since 1993 and he is very proud of the fact that he never left his village during all the years of war.

'Rwandans, Burundians, Mai Mai – I've seen them all. I am like a whore', he laughs.

At Dine, on the other side of the bay, it is a completely different story. Internal squabbles over the chieftaincy have caused strife in the community and, leaderless, they seem unsure what to do. The new chief is not popular, so the crowds that greet us on the beach introduce us to the former one. He is not as blasé as his colleague across the bay and he admits running away from Dine because of war four times: in 1964, 1977, 1996 and 2002. Now Dine is a ruin. His father came here in 1946, when the peninsula was a national park, and started a colony of fishermen. His father pressed the Belgians to allow them to stay and make it a village.

'Ahh, that's when Dine was really Dine!' remembers the former chief.

Now, most of the gaunt and eager-looking people clustered around our little bench are returnees and they are hungry. They have started farming but the yield is not good. The cassava that they planted is diseased and they must gather what they can from the forest. People are surviving on very little. One woman unfolds her palm to show me a collection of tiny palm nuts: 'This is what we give to the children so they won't go to sleep hungry', says the former chief.

The woman dutifully demonstrates how she will crack the nut and grind it into powder. Mixed with water, it will make a paste that will fill the belly of her child, to create an illusion of fullness and stop the baby crying for a while. Dine's inhabitants are simply waiting; waiting for food, for tools, for fishing nets, for tin roofs for their houses. When we leave, they wave frail hands in front of mournful faces, sorry to see another hope disappearing.

'Did you not bring any goats this time?' asks the former chief.

Night folds the people of Dine into its shadows and we motor back across the bay to Mizimu to sleep. I want to sleep on the beach with the crew. Mashine and Gilet think this is a splendid idea, a vote of confidence in their way of life but Bienvenue is having none of it. He says it would be a terrible insult not to sleep with the people of the village.

'The crew are people of the water. They are used to sleeping by the lake, not like you', he informs me. 'The crew have magic that keeps them safe. They can defeat crocodiles with their magic. But you cannot. It would be too dangerous.'

Instead I must share a bed in one of the mud huts with Bienvenue, who wriggles like a five-year-old. I would have preferred to risk the crocodiles.

The following day we stop at several villages to deliver sewing machines to the returned refugees and to ask about the goats that were delivered last time. At a place called Mwajenga, as I loll with the crew in the shade, Yvette comes over to tell us that Bienvenue is delayed because of some problem with the goats. Apparently, they have all died from a mysterious disease. Judging by Yvette's arched eyebrows, she doesn't quite believe it.

At our next stop, Mwindo, it is the same story. Dozens of goats are roaming across the beach but the residents tell Bienvenue that they are not the ones that he delivered last time. The ones delivered by the UN all died from a strange disease. Something doesn't add up but Bienvenue cannot be bothered to argue. He is in a rush to reach Kazimiya before nightfall; there waits the promise of a bed in a concrete house, beer, running water and maybe even a television.

When it is time to leave Mwindo, Bienvenue is still noisily unloading the parts of a sewing machine from the boat. He is wearing starched white shorts with a leather belt, and two-tone shoes. With his guilty eyes and sad expression, he looks more like an Italian mobster than a humanitarian worker. In an imperious voice, he assures the old men on the shore that all the pieces of the sewing machine are there. By the way they busy themselves assembling it right on the beach, I suspect they do not believe him; they want to discover if anything is missing before we leave. As the men on the shore become increasingly frantic, Bienvenue shouts to Mashine to go. The engine bursts into sudden life and with a throaty rattle of the motor we are off again.

A little girl pulls off her dress, runs into the lake, and swims alongside the boat. As she swims, she sings, a song wishing us well along our way. Her beautiful voice hangs in the air as I watch the men struggling with their sewing machine, losing screws in the sand.

It is getting dark. We race against the fading light to reach Kazimiya, the only harbour for many miles. The surface of the lake is occasionally thick with patches of crude oil that bubbles up naturally from fissures underwater; wealth simply floating on the water, waiting to be harvested. But the war has prevented any oil exploration or drilling. It is unbearably wrong, a lake full of fish and fuel, surrounded by starving villagers with not enough to eat.

We arrive in Kazimiya in the dark. The crew want me to stay and eat with them but Yvonne and Bienvenue insist I join them at their friend's house. The sailors accept this commonplace discrimination without a word but, in the morning, Mashine tells how they stayed awake all night terrified, watching crocodiles coming ashore. We all laugh. No one suggests that they should have slept in the house with us; it is taken for granted that their place is in the boat.

The next morning, we set off late. Bienvenue and Yvette pull as many excuses as possible so they can continue watching television, delaying our departure. After half an hour, they are cursing their decision to set off at all. The waves rise quickly; the sky turns a cold hard grey and the wind whips spray over the bow. The crew are worried, their voices rise and then their chatter stops completely; a bad sign.

Mashine aims the boat for a gap in the marshy reeds on the lakeshore. As we approach, a man standing knee-deep in the shallows waves his arms and shouts directions. Others appear, waving and yelling. As we make the gap and fasten the boat, the people on the shore crowd around and want to know where we are going. Mashine senses that they want something and he remains non-committal.

We follow them up a short track to a small mud-and-grass hut tucked underneath a big tree. In the lee of the house twenty people – several men and women and about a dozen children – huddle on a UNICEF tarpaulin.

They have come from Baraka. There is no more land, no space to farm, and everyone there is hungry. They have heard that in Talama there is land and plenty of food. They have walked for four days but the path ends at Kazimiya. After that, as I have discovered myself, the lake is the only way south and now they are looking for a lift. They plead and plead with Mashine but Bienvenue is adamant: the insurance won't allow it, he claims. Insurance? In Congo?

When the weather calms, and we ready ourselves to board the boat, the best I can do is to leave them some pasta and tins of tuna (from the Seychelles) and some lollipops for the children. As we walk away down the path, one of the men runs after me: he wants to know what the pasta is and how to prepare it.

'Sorry for my ignorance', he says.

Under way again, the sky is clear and the placated lake sparkles in the afternoon sun, coyly apologetic that it could have ever been menacing and threatening. The sorry refugees are left behind and we continue south, down past the rebel coast. It is many days to Kalemie, and that is only halfway down the lake. At this rate, to reach the southernmost port, Moba, and then to turn inland towards Manono seems like an improbable feat, a very long way indeed. The swathe of imposing hills and valleys on our right is endless, impenetrable. Here, in the 1960s, Che Guevara and Laurent Kabila planned their abortive attempt to organize a rebel army against the dictator Mobutu. Forty years later, the valleys remain the site of rebel activity: Bwalile trained here with Dunya, during the recent war.

In the afternoon light, the town of Yungu appears, perched on the side of a mountain range that tumbles into the water from a great height. There, I accompany Bienvenue to see the chief who is reportedly also not happy about the goats – there are not enough of them to go around. His office is painted avocado and a huge commemorative portrait of the recent wedding of President Kabila and his wife adorns one wall.

'You can't help some people and not others', he complains. 'I get people coming from the other villages saying that they too want sewing machines and goats. It is causing grave problems for the *sous-chefferie*.'

Bienvenue pleads innocence. It is the UN that decides things, he says, and no one can ever understand them, of course.

'What about those goats anyway?' asks Bienvenue.

'They died from a strange disease', says the chief.

'But what about all these other goats I see in the village, they did not suffer from the disease?' asks Bienvenue.

'No, well, of course, they are *adapté* to the environment here, the environment is harsh, you see', explains the chief.

Yungu is in fact a paradise, for humans and for goats: it has a temperate climate and rich brown soil and is crisscrossed with crystal streams that fall off the mountains. Nevertheless, all the UN goats seem to have met the same fate. Later that evening, Bienvenue's friends reveal what really happened. When the charity's plan encountered the reality of post-war Congo, the goats did not stand a chance.

The beneficiaries of the scheme did not see the point of planning to eat one goat in a year's time, possibly, if the goat survived. This being Congo, one cannot be sure of anything. In a place where no one knows where the next meal is coming from, it makes more sense to eat one goat now. A bird in the hand is worth two in the bush. In Swahili, there is a similar saying: *Ngombe ya maskini hazai* – the poor man's cow does not give birth. So accustomed are the Congolese to misfortune that they diminish expectations before they have even started to hope. Better to simply stoke up the fire and roast the goat while you can.

In Yungu, time moves slowly. The morning is all noise and then, around three or four, when shadows begin to slide from the mountains and the water quiets to glass, people turn to strolling; feet that slapped down to the water's edge at dawn now swing languidly towards the promise of evening satisfaction. Whatever happens in this, the hour of the day's turning, will stay longer in the memory, pressed on the soul like a flower in a book, preserved in intricate detail.

In the long afternoon, people lounge in the shade, facing the lake. Since I am waiting for Bienvenue and Yvette to drag themselves away from their friends in Yungu and head on south, under the trees is the appropriate place for me, too. There is no road on which to watch passers-by; the only access is by boat or along a mountain path that leads to the mining town of Ngalula. Among those dozing under the thin casuarina trees, listening to stray Tanzanian radio signals from across the lake, are gold traders waiting for a boat. Yungu is a quiet place and thus perfect for smuggling gold.

'We've been waiting for three days', explains Pipi, one of the well-dressed men sitting in the shade. Recently returned from Tanzania, he has the hesitancy and the politeness of the refugee. Pipi brings gold from the mines at Ngalula through the mountains to Yungu, a journey of about two days on foot, with his nights spent sleeping on the path. He has heard of Manono, further to the west, but he has never been there.

'You can't carry tin', he says.

He unfurls a small cloth bag gingerly; inside is a handful of dust. It looks like a spice: it is fifty thousand dollars' worth of gold. All the small traders contribute and hire a boat to cross the lake to Kigoma in Tanzania together. They must hide the gold well from the Tanzanian authorities to avoid paying tax. To the Congolese authorities, they pay nothing.

'They are afraid of us. They are only a few and we are many. That is why Yungu is good for smuggling.'

Sometimes they carry more, sometimes less. A few weeks ago, Pipi and his friends came back with two billion Tanzanian shillings among thirty men. Almost two million dollars. This is a drop in the lake: eighty per cent of Congo's riches are smuggled out of the country. As a small insight into this illicit world, in 2011 four hundred kilos of gold, about twenty-three million dollars' worth, were seized by police from a private jet in Goma. Those allegedly involved were senior Congolese government officials, a Kenyan customs officer, and a Houston-based Nigerian diamond merchant who spent a month under house arrest in a hotel in Goma before being released. The gold later went missing.

'If it were not for the war, this country would be rich', Pipi says, proudly.

But it seems to me it is actually the war that has enabled him and his friends to get rich. The war has kept at bay the companies with the technology to put the miners out of work, the multi-nationals who have more sophisticated ways of avoiding tax and accessing global transport networks that will make obsolete the rocky footpath to the mines and the small wooden boats that cross the lake. Instead, the gold will find its way to Rwanda and then to Europe in aeroplanes and trucks and those who get rich will sit in offices in Kinshasa and Kigali, not here in Yungu on benches in the hot sun, waiting for a leaky boat. I know I probably shouldn't but I hope for his sake that the multi-nationals don't show up any time soon.

Our quiet afternoon is shattered, when, with a shout, Bienvenue bounds down to the shore to rouse the crew from the boat's hull where they've been sleeping off the afternoon. With a flurry, we bundle into our boat just in time to reach Talama, another sleepy village, before nightfall. That evening a television is hooked up to a generator and two hundred children watch a Nigerian soap opera in English. They understand nothing. Instead, they maintain a constant conversation about what may or may not be happening as they characters play out their mime show. In a place where not long ago these settlements were deserted, it is a joy to hear them laugh.

Once again, my plans to sleep on the beach are scotched by Yvette and Bienvenue. It is my last chance to spend the night with the crew, for tomorrow they are turning back and I will be on my own. Yvette points me to a room, more fitting to my status, but where a goat stands on the roof, attached by a rope. It bleats through the night like a child being tortured. In the morning, I ask our host if the goat was donated by the UN.

'Ah, *non*, you know, those ones were not well suited to the environment, they all died.'

I think I detect a faint smile on his lips.

14

A cruise on Tanganyika

Fela, Punk, and Captain push the pirogue on Lake Tanganyika

IT IS TIME TO say goodbye to the *Nyota ya Bahari* and her wonderful circus of characters. The rocky, remote and beautiful village of Talama is as far south as they will go. Somehow I've got to find my way over one hundred kilometres further down the coast, by water, alone.

Talama clings to the base of these mountains by an act of will. There are paths up into the hills and to the towns beyond but that would take many days of hard walking and divert me from the lakeside villages that I have come to see. The only other way out is to hire a pirogue, the ancient dugouts that have plied this lake for centuries. There are several on the steeply shelving beach at Talama, pulled up above the waterline. Occasionally, overloaded cargo boats visit this coast but mostly the inhabitants just paddle, or 'push', as they say in Swahili.

Gilet reckons it's a day's push to Wimbi, the next village along the coast and from there, maybe two or three to Kabimba, a larger town where, if I'm lucky, there might be other transport. If not, however, it is another three or more days of paddling to Kalemie, the place the Belgians called Albertville, founded in 1894, named after King Leopold's son. Kalemie is the half-way point down the lake. There, I shall need to find a commercial craft going south for the rest of the way down. I'm hopeful, because the town is Tanganyika's largest port.

Until Kalemie, however, there's no guarantee that anyone will want to ferry me onwards, only a vague assumption that people need money and the hope that a boat can always be found. I am on a cruise into the unknown.

Bwalile, Mashine, and Gilet are quiet. One by one they give me a hug and wish me well. They have become my family. I feel we could sail in the *Nyota ya Bahari* all the way down the lake, along the Lukuga to the Congo and off around the world without a second thought, so natural has the daily rhythm of sailing, swimming and eating become.

'Don't hire anyone from Shaba. Those people can't be trusted', says Gilet.

He thinks the inhabitants of Katanga province – *Shaba* in Swahili, meaning copper, its principal export – are all thieves and rapists. Gilet and Mashine have approved the crew of my pirogue and the amount that I am paying them for the first leg to Wimbi.

Yvette and Bienvenue shake my hand formally. Bienvenue pleads for me to go back with them; he thinks this plan is the height of insanity and that he will be fired for allowing me to go. Gilet and Bwalile help launch the boat. As we push into the clear blue afternoon, they wave from the shore. The paddlers break into a rhythmic song and I wave back from astride my little bench in the middle. I feel ridiculous, like a colonial relic. The only thing missing is a white pith helmet.

Wimbi means 'wave' in Swahili. Fortunately, today there aren't any. Six hours later, the paddlers silent and drenched in sweat, we arrive in the fading light. The paddlers beach the pirogue to let me off, then promptly turn around to push the six hours back again in the dark. I, meanwhile, walk up the shore into the waiting arms of the authorities, unsure what to expect.

The deputy chief is a large man with a sour face. He is taken aback by my arrival; it's just his luck that a strange visitor should arrive when he is standing in for the real chief. He receives me in his compound, a low fence surrounding about ten square feet of muddy ground. Hundreds of villagers chatter, and poke their faces above the fence, well aware that he has no idea what to do with me. He takes me into a corner and appraises me sternly while I imagine all sorts of nasty outcomes. But, as ever, Congo is more hospitable than hostile.

'We would be honoured to have you as our guest in Wimbi. We will arrange a place for you to stay. There is just one problem' – he lowers his voice so the crowd can't hear – 'What do you eat?'

If there is one thing that even those in remote villages know, it is that white people cannot possibly eat the same food as Africans. When I do finally sit down hours later and join them in eating maize meal with my hands, they are delighted, the more so that I have confounded their expectations. After dinner, the deputy chief summons the elders and we crowd into a little hut lit by a single candle. I am exhausted and desperate for sleep but this is the hour for business. They will help me find a boat onwards but first I must hear their complaints. Wimbi gets few visitors, and they ask that I carry their pleas to the UN, the international community, the outside world.

Later, the chief shows me to a single-storey brick house with a tin roof, a floor of swept mud, and broken sacks of dried maize slumped in the corner. A couple of planks have been laid on the floor: this is my bed. I spend the night wide awake, watching the rats scuttle over my sleeping bag on their way to the maize. Just before dawn, rain begins hammering on the roof and dripping all over the mud floor. I drag the sleeping bag and the planks into the only dry corner, next to the rats and the maize, and wait for the grey light.

Several hours later, the deputy chief arrives, with rolled-up trousers and muddy sandals. I must visit the village, and I must see everything, he says, so that I can tell others, important people, about the pitiful state of the town, made even more pitiful by the never-ending downpour.

First stop is the hospital. On the side of an empty concrete and tin shell with no windows and no doors is a small wooden sign, whose fading, hand-painted letters commemorate the names of the agencies that wrote cheques and then forgot about Wimbi and its needy patients. Opposite, a red cross hangs on the wall of a straw and mud hut: the real hospital.

Marian is a serious, stout woman with lively eyes, enormous heart-shaped earrings, and the air of someone in charge. She is the midwife. She was the midwife before the war, too. She stares at the lake and swats flies while explaining how things have deteriorated in Wimbi. A solar panel, forlornly collecting rain, powers the only electric light in the village, used for night operations. It was donated by a politician during the 2006 general election campaign. Marian sounds tired, aware that she is not performing the role the deputy chief expects of her.

'The school is better, you must visit the school', she says.

The school is a beacon of hope, a sign of what solidarity can achieve. The village has worked together to build new classrooms. There is just one problem: they could not get tin sheets for the roof, so when it rains, like today, school is cancelled and the walls, made of mud, disintegrate.

Right now, the rain looks as though it will never end. The town is composed of straw and mud huts that are rapidly returning to raw materials. Everything is disintegrating. Though some solid mud-brick buildings pepper the streets, they are few. The villagers have been forced to re-build their houses so many times that they will not bother to make permanent structures again until they are sure of the peace. There are 3600 people living in this makeshift town but before the war there were fifteen thousand.

'Every family has lost someone', says the deputy chief 'and others are still too afraid to come back'.

He indicates a mango tree where, he claims, Laurent Kabila announced, with Che, his first revolution against the government.

'Do you know about Che Guevara, the white man? Would you like to meet his friend?'

'Of course.'

We go to a mud compound that looks like any other, except there is an armed guard by the gate. After paying an entrance fee denominated in cigarettes, we go into a slightly grander mud hut, where an old man lies, wheezing, on a wooden bench underneath a purple curtain. He trained with Kabila and Che Guevara in the 1960s, although he can't remember much about Che, apart from his cigars. He joined the revolution back then because he was tired of soldiers harassing people and demanding money when they didn't have identity cards. Not much has changed.

'There were seven reasons why our revolution failed', he announces, but manages to list only three before his hand falls on the bed and he lets out a long sigh that ends in a rattle and a wheeze: Che and the rebels had no discipline, they forgot about the suffering of the people and they drank too much.

'Just like the army today', I laugh.

But the old man doesn't laugh. He is a friend of the young president and he is optimistic.

'Joseph will accomplish what his father could not', he says confidently and stares out of the doorway of his hut. The old man is too tired to talk; what he really wants, from me, is malarial medicine for himself and his sick wife. We venture out and buy him some and then must bribe the soldier again to deliver it.

'And now can we go and see the pirogue?' I ask the deputy chief.

'Yes, yes', he ignores me warmly, 'let us eat'.

The only restaurant in town is another leaky mud hut with four small benches. Steam rises from a kettle atop a brazier in the doorway. The owner is a supremely hospitable woman and her tea and doughnuts are hot. Few people have money here; we are the only customers. After several minutes, two young men come in who, by the look of their sports shoes and intact t-shirts, are better-off than most. The older and fatter one is telling his companion about the wood business. I stare out at the rain, try to ignore the chief's conversation and eavesdrop.

In summary: you can get a permit to log the forests in Katanga for ten dollars and for this you can log anywhere, as much as you like. Boats go to Kigoma in Tanzania several times a week carrying timber from Congo. In Kigoma, the buyers pay five dollars a board, and one tree contains about fifteen to twenty boards. That means you only need to chop one tree to cover the cost of the permit, a great business.

'If only one can raise the money for the permit, you could do well indeed', says the older man. The younger one looks on, wide-eyed.

This must be the reason that the steep wooded hills above the village, dropping down into the lake, and the ones that we passed on the way here, are scarred with brown streaks where forest used to be. The ridgeline above

Wimbi is decorated with odd trees, like a young wispy moustache. Gone is the thick crown of forest that would once have adorned it.

After lunch we finally go to inspect the boat that the deputy chief has arranged for me. My ride is a sad little craft, empty, awaiting its crew. Inscribed along the inside of the hull is the legend, *Acheni fitina – siyo mimi ni Mungu amenipangia*: 'Stop your jealousy – it is not my doing but God who has blessed me'. A pirogue is a hefty piece of capital, to be envied.

The deputy chief hurries off to round up the crew and returns, apologetically, with a bunch of schoolboys. They are young and rowdy and already complaining before they have even climbed into the boat. This is going to be a painful trip.

'Kabimba is far, we will get there at night. You white man, you will pay us extra when we get there', says one.

'We'll see.'

The chief makes me promise to make the boys return as soon as possible; they should not miss more than two days of school.

Kabimba is a full day's push. Because of the rain we set off late: only two hours of light remain. The boys are right; we will get there in the dark, if indeed we get there at all tonight. The going is slow. The boys talk and joke but seem unable to row and talk at the same time. The two younger ones do all the work and the two older ones, Joseph and 'Punk', smoke cigarettes and make jokes; no amount of stern talk can motivate them to row. Even once it gets dark, they don't seem to be in a hurry.

With the darkness comes a drop in the breeze. The water is like oil and the stars that pop out one by one float on the surface of the lake. At first the mountains turn mauve in the dusk, and then black against the velvet sky, until finally they merge and it is impossible to make out where the lake meets the shore, or where the wall of hills ends and the heavens begin. When the chop and swish of the paddles breaks for a while, the silence is huge and a little frightening. Every now and then, the pinprick of an oil lamp is visible in a village on the shore but for long stretches the land is simply dark, black, asleep.

We push on through the night and the conversation among the rowers keeps up its frivolous pace. They want girlfriends, preferably from abroad; a ticket out of Congo. They argue about the best place to find mud to build bricks back in Wimbi. They all want to build their own home out of fired mud bricks, not grass and straw, which crumbles in the rain.

Joseph suggests that they lie and say that the trip took longer than expected, so that they can stay another night in Kabimba, away from home. There they can drink beer, maybe try and find some girls, for they don't get a chance like this very often and they feel no loyalty to the owner of the pirogue. It turns out he has paid them half of what he charged me for their services and they are pissed off. There are no secrets in a village.

Everything I do or say is fascinating to the boys. When I read a book by torchlight, their chatter stops immediately; we sit in silence, me reading, and four pairs of eyes in the dark watching me read. Since the war, books are rare. The boys grew up in refugee camps, in Tanzania, where they went to the free schools. They say they'd like to continue with their studies after they finish school in Wimbi but their talk lacks conviction; they seem to believe this plan is nothing but a conversation piece, and without education they will probably never leave the village.

Joseph has shrunk his dreams to fit his circumstances. Almost. 'I don't want to live anywhere but Congo. But I would like to see Europe just once', he says, sounding unconvinced.

They get tired paddling. I take over from each of them in turn. We've been pushing in the dark for hours but still, Kabimba is far away. There is an argument about how far it is. 'Captain', the smallest and possibly the youngest, maybe thirteen or fourteen, thinks it is too far to reach tonight. The darkness is weighing on us. Fela, a quiet diligent boy, and Captain reckon they know where we are by the merest shadow on the hills. Fela is sure the village of Kalala is around the next bay. It is already ten o'clock and when I ask if we will reach Kabimba this evening, there is silence. No one wants to admit that they will not deliver me tonight. Okay, I tell them, we will stay at Kalala and continue in the morning. This elicits grunts of agreement and urgency returns to their paddling; the end in sight.

After an hour of pushing round the headland, we still cannot see a thing but Captain guides us towards the looming black mass of shore. His knowledge of the bay is amazing. The pirogue lurches with each stroke of our paddles and we manoeuvre between other canoes, moored by strings slung from the beach. Then, with a bump, the front hits sand. In the circle of my torch, the water is filthy, awash with rubbish.

We pull the boat up on to the mud shore and knock on the door of the first house we find. It is nearly midnight, and any self-respecting villager will be asleep. From inside, a weary voice tells us that the chief's house is on the other side of the village. Following protocol even at this hour, we quietly weave along alleyways, hop over open sewers and, at one point, balance on a log over a wide river teeming with rubbish, to introduce ourselves.

More knocking locates the house of the chief and, after an eternity, his wife opens the door. It is past midnight but his spirits are high, *'Jambo, Mzungu!'* – Hello, white man! – he greets me. He says we can sleep in the village guesthouse and bids us follow him. After the long push from Wimbi, the boys are like dogs finding dry land after a long voyage in confinement, running around, chasing each other and rolling on the ground. The chief worries that he should find us some mats or blankets for sleeping but Joseph reassures him: 'Don't worry, the wazungu, they have everything'. He is right: I do.

The next morning, I wake at five on the hard mud floor of the single-roomed mud house. A few feet away, the four boys lie in a row on a rough palm-frond mat; still in their clothes, they must be freezing. Joseph is hissing at me. He still doesn't know my name.

'Mzungu! Let's go.'

In the pink dawn, Kalala shows itself. Its little houses are made of mud and black granite and its paths are covered in fine black shale. A waterfall cuts the cliff above the town. Granite slabs have been arranged to create an overflow system for the river when it floods and most houses have a little terrace of granite and gravel. The black stone gives the place the feel of prehistoric time, a simple, golden age. The neat streets present a picture of happy orderliness, save that the hills are stripped bare: hardwoods are piled up on the beach, ready to be shipped out. The town smacks of leadership and confidence, as though pride in one's environment is the first line of defence against the devastation of war. Which, I suppose, it is.

The lake is smooth and the clouds scud across a crisp morning sky the fragile blue of a bird's egg. We paddle past three numbered villages: Kilozi I, II, and III. The inhabitants call out for us to stop and visit them but the boys are in a hurry, so we don't.

'Come and see "New Congo"', they call.

They are proud of their new settlements, built together by returning refugees of all tribes, the boys tell me. Survival here is a cosmopolitan struggle.

Another few hours and the lackadaisical boys eventually bring the pirogue into the port of Kabimba, a concrete gash in the lush forest, crowned with a cement factory belching smoke. The view is strange, a caricature of a swampy, feverish colonial dream. It is not much of a place but we are exhausted and thrilled to arrive, though, sure enough, even before the prow of the canoe has hit the muddy landing stage, two badly-dressed and malnourished men in fraying suits begin shouting at us from the shore:

'We are from the *Bureau de sécurité intérieure* and I am afraid you must come to our office right away!'

I tip the boys and tell them to head back as soon as they have had some food. They don't say anything but I catch Joseph and Punk grinning at each other.

Sleep. That is the only thing on my mind as I sit in the dingy office in the port while painfully, slowly, a naval official writes down all my details on scraps of paper, as the supply of official forms dried up years ago. He is called Adjutant Robert and he wants to chat. I give minimal answers and stare through the window.

'Ben. Student, Manono'

'You're going there?' he asks, then adds 'those people cannot be trusted'.

'Yes, yes', I murmur. I am sure that if I get to Manono, the people there will be just as charming as everyone else I have met but assent is my way out of Robert's paperwork. My stay in the villages has shown that Congolese hospitality is alive and well, even exhausting on occasions, as Robert is in the process of demonstrating.

The view through the window is dominated by a rusting, slightly listing crane on rails, which hangs like a hangman's noose over the dock. A ship is tethered to the dock; beyond it are another three in a row. People clamber from one to the next to reach the ship they want. All the ships look as though they have come to Kabimba to die a maritime death. The furthest and most decrepit ship of the bunch is a rusting hulk of a barge, the *Moba*.

'That is the boat you will take to Kalemie', says Robert. 'It leaves at four pm.'

I had hoped to stay a few days in Kabimba. An old lady in Yungu had given me a letter for her daughter, Dolores, who works in the migration office here. But Robert, with characteristic common sense, advises against lingering.

'You do not know when the next boat will leave.'

When I find Dolores, she agrees. She is an exception to my new rule; she is not keen for me to stay. She might have insisted, made a fuss, assured me that another boat would be along soon – that would be Congolese hospitality as I've come to know it. But no. Instead, she taps her pretty high-heeled shoes and bats her heavily made-up lashes: 'Robert is right, it is better if you travel today'. It seems her husband is away and making her the talk of the town would be unhelpful, so I humbly accept their advice and prepare to leave again.

Dolores's boss in the migration office is an intelligent man whose pressed shirt is completed by a row of neatly-ordered pens clipped into its top pocket. Despite the muddy chaos of Kabimba, he has shiny shoes. He is courteous in the extreme. It is a miracle that he manages to stay so urbane. At times, I am surprised that people haven't simply given up. Why bother going to work and wearing your uniform if you don't get paid? What's the point of wearing a smart shirt with gold-tipped pens and shiny shoes if you have to walk to work through flood-washed streets drowning in rubbish? But when that is all you have, it is all the more important. His personal appearance is a mark of disdain for the disaster that Congo has become. Like Kalala's ordered streets, self-respect, manners, hospitality are markers of hope, refusals to capitulate, to allow their high standards to become victims of the war.

After the formalities of the migration office, Adjutant Robert negotiates with the captain of the *Moba* so that I will pay nothing to travel to Kalemie. 'We don't get many tourists here – you are our guest', he insists.

Someone else carries my bag on to the deck. A fellow passenger offers me his chair, which he is transporting to Kalemie. At last, sleep might be mine. The air fills with the smell of roasting maize as the passengers on deck camp down for the night around little braziers and we wait for the tug-boat to pull this rusting hulk of a barge through the night to Kalemie. In any other country, this barge would be dissected for scrap metal or lying on the bottom of the sea.

A young man fetches me an ice-cold bottle of Primus. I haven't laundered my clothes in a week, slept properly for four days, washed for three or eaten for two. But now, with a cold beer and the gift of a chair, all is right with the world. I recline with my feet on the rail, high above the oily water of the harbour and, as I watch the sun disappear into the trees and listen to the sound of roosting birds squawking in the dusk, I toast the wonders of Congo; her tragedy, her beauty and, above all, her hospitality.

I snuggle down into my sleeping bag on the deck along with everyone else as the hubbub of Kabimba recedes and the chug of the diesel engine takes over. The stars come out; the sky is taut and clear, the skin of a drum. The sleep for which I have longed these last four days takes me like a thief, suddenly and swiftly, all at once.

15

The intelligence director's bath

Railway carriages rust in Kalemie

IT IS STILL DARK. The *Moba* is waiting to dock at Kalemie, once the east's major port, the end of the railway that Stanley built from the sea. From this town, Katanga province's grain, beer, timber and metals used to be shipped across Central Africa legitimately, paying taxes, of course. The port brought prosperity, making Kalemie the jewel of the lake: luxurious sleeper trains carried tourists through the jungle to the beaches by the lake. My pre-dawn arrival is not so glamorous, aboard a dilapidated wreck.

The door of one of the berths clangs open and a woman emerges carrying a bowl of water. She sets it down carefully and squats to light a brazier. As the water warms, she looks out at the lake. The sound of humans waking slowly gathers force. Two soldiers quietly murmur to each other while balancing their rifles on the twisted and broken handrail of the barge. Behind the squatting woman, there is an occasional quack from a duck trussed up on the floor of a small cupboard; somebody's luggage. When the water starts to bubble, the woman takes it off the heat, pours some into a bucket, and adds more cold. She stands up, unhurriedly undresses and deliberately washes herself on deck, in front of the rest of us, still wrapped in our blankets. After a while, a chorus of mobile phones starts up. Before six in the morning, calls are free, so for the poor this is a vital, if a little inhospitable, window.

Amid the wreckage of the commercial port, a brass band on the quayside plays a welcome for a boat full of refugees returning from Tanzania. No such welcome for me: I follow a round man called Pascale towards an old warehouse in which some cardboard partitions have been erected to make a little office for the *Direction générale de migration*. Each step of my journey must be noted, documented, stamped. The bureaucracy is an obstacle course.

A nervous thin man stamps my passport and welcomes me to Kalemie with a formal bow.

I trail Pascale across rusting train tracks, around which goats graze, past train carriages with smashed windows and towards row upon row of hollow and faded colonial buildings. One, a little less hopeless than the rest, has a sign above the door: 'Health Office'.

Pascale's job is to protect the people of Kalemie from strangers unwittingly bringing epidemics into the municipality. Never mind that Kalemie has plenty of its own. Unfortunately for him, the door to his office is locked and he has no key so he agrees to take my vaccination card and deliver it to me later at the Hotel du Lac, where, in a delusional moment, I decided to treat myself after this gruelling cruise.

In the port's busy heyday, the Hotel du Lac was Kalemie's grandest hotel. Tall white columns of peeling paint face a boulevard that curves elegantly along the lakeshore. I peer in through the broken windows and heave open the heavy door, to find no one at the solid teak reception desk. The lounge contains the remains of two overpolished mahogany sofas upholstered in cracked orange leather. The grand stairway opens impressively on to a generous lobby tiled in red, where ball gowns and dinner suits once thronged.

After much shouting, someone comes and I am assigned a room. There is no running water and the beds are dusty but the old orderlies are sweet and generous. They smile at me kindly as they patrol the corridors in faded green uniforms and bare feet.

The town, like the hotel, is broken; it has no industry. The Coca-Cola comes from Tanzania and the beer from

Zambia. The grand high street is lined with crumbling white facades and coconut trees. Everything stands monument to the colonial theft of Congo's resources and Mobutu's mismanagement.

A few minutes after I have flung my filthy bag on the floor and wrenched open the rusting doors to the balcony, there is a knock. The thin man from the *Migration* is at the door, flustered. He wants me to go back to his office at the port because his boss has not 'seen' me.

'What do you mean he has not "seen" me?' I ask.

'*Mon chef*, he does not have confidence in me', the officer apologizes.

'So? That's not my problem', I say. 'Did I not fill in all the required forms?'

'*Oui, mais …*'

'Tell your *chef* that I refuse to come.' I listen to him plead and then order and then shout, until I tire of the lobbying and shut the door. Translated, he has been reprimanded for not getting some cash out of me.

It happens that the director of the intelligence services, the dreaded ANR, keeps a suite at the Hotel du Lac, and he is roused by the noise. He shouts at the officer and then apologizes to me. 'You are quite right to refuse. It is a disgrace, this cheap harassment for the sake of a few francs. But what is the cost to our reputation when we treat visitors in such a way?'

He says it as though tourists were a common occurrence and not, like me, a freak accident, as though the damage done would ruin the economy.

V.S. Naipaul, writing about colonialism in South America, said:

> Empire damaged us ... It kept us backward, gave us very little to do. It gave us as men no way of proving ourselves. It never made us believe in human achievement. It made us believe only in luck and birth and influence and theft and getting patents from the King. It made us cringe before authority and mock it at the same time. It made us believe that all men at bottom are worthless ... It was ten years before I understood that things were different in other countries.

Belgian rule seems to have had a similar effect in Kalemie and the cities of Congo, the places where colonial life took strongest root.

The residue of colonialism has engendered cruelty, brutality and a lack of confidence in any African achievement or even any African idea of humanity. What is it to be a man? Only money. There is no value in honour, respect or social standing. Perhaps there is in the villages. But here, in this broken town, no one seems able to imagine that life might be different or different elsewhere; that people do not daily try to rob each other blind and still remain friends.

Later, Pascale arrives at the appointed time and we have a beer. I buy him cigarettes and chat about his salary: ten dollars a month. He has lived in Kalemie his whole life. He has a wife and too many children. Like all good Congolese nationalists, he hates the Banyamulenge. Eventually, I ask for the document that he has brought but not as yet released from his breast pocket. It looks increasingly at risk from the ring of sweat spreading from under his arm. Without those papers, I cannot leave. Any petty official has the power to ruin my plan and send me home at whim.

'Of course', he says, as though the card is a trifle and not the reason he is here. 'There is just the small matter of the fee for the ink of the stamp. It is ten dollars.'

'What?' I can't believe that he is going to try and rob me after several beers and cigarettes. Not to mention that the locked office was his problem. I am determined to stand firm. 'I know the law, Pascale. I don't want to end up in jail for bribing you.'

He is embarrassed and capitulates too soon.

'I understand. I'm sorry. It is just that my boss will think that I have stolen the money.'

Together we think of a way out of this unfortunate situation: the illegal, corrupt nature of his boss. I agree to ask the head of security in the hotel to phone his superior and explain that the difficult foreigner has refused to pay anyone. Pascale looks doubtful. However, he hands over the vaccination card, duly stamped. Suddenly, with the awkward business out of the way, he asks where we are going dancing tonight and when he can come to pick me up and show me around town. It is as though another person has slipped into his uniform. The menacing public official has become the genial host, a common switch that I am coming to appreciate from Congo's troubled civil service. I cringe and mock them, like Naipaul, in equal measure.

The stairs have become a waterfall, cascading down four floors and making a small pond in the lobby; the Hotel du Lac becoming itself a lake. I splash upstairs to find my room an inch deep in water, pouring from a pipe hanging from the bathroom ceiling. Outside, on the landing, Paul, an orderly, is frantically sandbagging the top of the stairs.

Water is creeping out from under all the doors and the whole hotel is shaking with the rattling of pipes.

'I'm sorry, *Bwana* Ben, this always happens when we turn the water on. The intelligence director wanted a bath, so we had to turn it on but the pipes leak.' Now Paul and three others must mop up the water pouring down the corridors, while the intelligence director reclines in his bath.

16

The forest people

Batwa villagers smoking from ceremonial long pipes

BEFORE THE BELGIANS CAME to Congo in search of timber, rubber and metal, before the Banyamulenge migrated south from Rwanda, even before the Zanzibaris harvested slaves from these lands, eastern Congo was almost completely wooded and the people who lived there were the forest people: the Batwa, the pygmies. As the forest has retreated west to make way for cattle, roads, mines and cities, the Batwa have been given no place in the various visions for Congo's future, whether expounded by Belgians, Mobutu or the Kabilas.

The largest Batwa communities are in the forests of Ituri, in the far north, but there are some here in Katanga, not far from Kalemie. Before continuing south, I want to see how they are getting on, if they are returning to the forest after the war, if indeed any forest remains. I had heard stories about a man in Kalemie, Georges, who fights for Batwa rights; I want to meet him. For a day or so, I wonder how to find this man? I've heard he's short: one short man in a city of thousands, with only his first name to go on. How many men called Georges can there be in Kalemie? But Congo isn't like that.

After a damp night in the Hotel du Lac, I go to the first human rights organisation I can find, 'Human Dignity in the World' (HDW), located on a sandy back street in Kalemie. The worker who opens the door knows my man.

'Georges! Of course we know Georges.'

Word spreads that there is a visitor and soon the head of HDW arrives. He is a tall, welcoming man and, strangely for the head of a human rights organisation, a veterinary surgeon. The others refer to him simply as 'Doctor'. Moments after they telephone him, Georges arrives, on the back of a motorbike, in a cloud of dust. This is to become a familiar sight. He is indeed small.

'Is he Batwa?' I ask the doctor.

'No, he's just short.'

Georges's organisation is called *Voix des minorités indigenes* (VMI). Georges may be short and softly-spoken but his is an emphatic voice in a place where few want to talk about Batwa rights, a place where the word for 'human' and the words used to describe these diminutive people are different.

'The Congolese believe there are three kinds of people', the doctor explains, 'Muntus – normal people – Tutsis and pygmies'.

Georges is concerned about reports that Batwa are forbidden from mining at new gold and coltan sites in their territory, several hundred kilometres west of Kalemie. He wants me to see the discrimination at first hand. And so we plan a trip to the forest, a detour of several days from the lake and the route south but one that I enthusiastically embrace.

'Can you believe', he says furiously, 'there are still humans who consider other humans not humans?'

This is, apparently, what the chief of Kisengo said, where one of the off-limits mines is sited. In another nearby area, the chief of Benze has issued a directive to his people: 'If you see a Batwa on the road, kill him.'

I agree to meet Georges later to discuss logistics and head off to the UN compound for lunch. There, a large, chain-smoking Frenchman greets me. He has set up a charity here and runs it himself. When I recount the tale of the Hotel du Lac, he laughs. 'Never ever stay at the Hotel du Lac. Everybody in Kalemie knows that.'

He takes pity on me and invites me to stay in his compound instead and in the evening, some guys from another NGO come by for drinks. They speak the frontier language of the humanitarian world, peppered with acronyms and concerns about whether a place or a road or a project is *'bien securisé'*. They carry two-way radios that crackle and purr on the table among the beers, for they have to check in and out with their *chef de securité* every time they leave *le base*. It must be exhausting.

They are prisoners of the fiction that Congo, all of Congo, is a terribly dangerous place, to justify these ludicrous procedures and their sense of themselves as daring people. The situation is not so bad, however, as to prevent them from water-skiing on the lake at the weekend.

Two of the NGO workers have recently returned from Kisengo and the coltan mine. A cholera outbreak claimed two hundred lives there two weeks ago and, seemingly unaware of the irony, they try to persuade me not to visit the place: 'If you go to Kisengo, you'll die'.

I ignore their advice and, the next morning at six, Georges and two boys clatter into the NGO compound, revving their engines loudly. The drivers of our motorbikes are called Tonton and Tintin. What a pair! Tonton and Tintin's idea of alleviating the tedium of driving the long distance is to constantly overtake each other on the road while hurling insults over their shoulders.

The road climbs out of Kalemie through scrub. The forest has long since retreated and from the top of the hills we can see the province of Katanga stretching away from us, bigger than most European countries. This province was a country in its own right for a few brief years in the 1960s. Here and there, a lonely, unfeasibly tall tree has

escaped the axe; the scrub is the reason the Batwa are settling in villages: their forest habitat is disappearing.

The first wretched village we come to is Kabolu,
though it is really only half a village, a poor suburb of the
main village of Kabolu, where the Muntu, the 'normal'
people, live. We sit on sawn coconut logs and about fifty
men and women press round.

'Why is the village split in half?' I ask.

'Because we are pygmies', one man responds.

'The Muntu think we are animals. We are not people
like them.'

They all want to tell their stories at once. Two women
complain that they work all day in the fields of the Muntu
in exchange for enough cassava flour to feed a family one
meal. They don't have iron tools so they cannot grow food
for themselves. To buy tools, they need money but they are
never paid in cash, only in flour. It is a form of slave labour
and the lack of tools keeps them captive. The men tell me
how they used to hunt animals in the forest for food but
they hardly find any animals these days so they have taken
to gathering fruits and berries. Above all, hunger, hunger.

Their rising voices, one after another, offer a typical
morality tale of 1960s Africa, in which the rural villager is
lured to the town by the bright lights only to find that life
there is much harder than he thought. The Batwa have
been forced to abandon one way of life, only to find that
the new way of life they are seeking is out of reach.

They started going to church because they were told
that the white people would bring them clothes. 'Have you
brought any clothes for us?' asks one young man. It's true,
everyone is dressed in rags. I ask what was wrong with their
old dress, the bark and skins of the forest.

'There are many traditions that are changing. We must modernize', says an old man. He points at an old woman who looks as though she has only just survived a machete attack; a deep scar runs right down the middle of her forehead. 'We no longer do scarification on girls' faces, like that, or on their stomachs. When that old woman was a little girl, if you did not have scars, then you were not beautiful.'

The old woman offers a toothless grin.

'The Muntu women say we are ugly anyway. They say I am dirty, that I am not dressed and that they cannot eat from the same plate as me.'

That did not stop the Muntu men snatching Batwa girls. The Batwa have long survived by working for the Muntu and the Muntu, in return, take advantage of them.

'Discrimination is on the rise, though', says the man, 'because now they do not even come to steal our women and rape them, like they used to'.

Tonton and Tintin hate sitting still. As soon as we are back on the sandy gravel road, they resume their competition. Georges, in a black nylon jacket, a baseball cap pulled low and dark glasses to shield his eyes from the choking dust, clings to the back of the bike. We bounce and swerve along the snaking jungle paths in a teary blur. Before long, Georges raises his hand and indicates for us to stop at a place called Kasala-Nyumba.

Before we even sit down, the Muntu chief has heard of our arrival and puts himself at the centre of the crowd. The Batwa make way for him and provide a stool.

Alone, surrounded by sullen, hungry Batwa faces, he delivers his curious view of a curious history that is supposed to explain why the Muntu are justified in lording it over their shorter brothers.

'Just like the blacks have always worked for you whites, so the tradition of the pygmies has always been to work for the Muntu', he begins. Then his logic slips: 'If I am bigger than you, and if you want to better yourself and you have more money than me, will you still respect me?' So the tradition, he says, is that the Batwa are inferior to the Muntu.

Georges takes issue with him, provoking murmurs of support from the Batwa around us. 'You are the one who needs to modernise, not them', he says. 'Remember that the pygmies are the first Congolese; they were here before anyone else.'

The chief is unmoved, unashamed, surrounded by Batwa, some of whom are taller than him. He sits on his small wooden stool, holding court, with the Batwa ringing him, frowning. In a flash, they could overpower this little, arrogant man but they don't, they just stand there in their rags, mute, angry, humiliated. Enslaved.

When the Muntu chief leaves, Georges stands in the circle and addresses the crowd. He talks about his mini-census project: he wants the Batwa to make a record of who lives in their village. Some parts of Congo are regressing, modern life is in retreat, but other parts, like here, never experienced education, democracy or government in the first place.

'Is there anyone here who can read and write?' he asks.

There is much looking at the ground until one man, with reddish hair and bright eyes, is roughly pushed to the front. He is the only literate person in a village of at least four hundred homes.

'His father saw far', says someone in the crowd, by way of explanation.

'He helped us vote. We think we marked our thumbs for Kabila but many of us couldn't be sure.'

We race through the trees in the afternoon and reach the village of Kabala just as the sun is setting. Below a ridge, the Lukuga River stretches before us like a reptile snatching the last rays of the sun. The Lukuga is one of the main tributaries of the Congo River, and here measures fifty metres across. We wash in the warm brown water, perched on the wide grey rocks of the bank.

'Keep an eye out for crocodiles', says Georges with a twinkle. I barely care; it is such a relief to get the dust out of my hair, out of every wrinkle of skin. I feel like a pastry rolled in flour.

On top of the ridge, in the Muntu half of Kabala village, a Batwa dance is in full flow. Part of the tradition of superiority is that the Batwa dance for the Muntu when requested; mostly, however, they don't mind, for they like dancing. A young man with a bare chest, his head wrapped in straw, stamps his feet and shakes his raffia skirt intensely. His headdress is made of banana leaves and covers his face completely, like a teenage fringe or rocker's mane. Without eyes, without human features, he is transformed. For the Batwa, this figure whirling and steaming in the firelight is no longer a person but a genie, a spirit. His every move is mimicked by two girls, not more than twelve years old.

When he retreats from the circle, so do they. When he returns into the fray with a whoop and a double-footed stamp that sends the bells on his ankles wild, they follow.

The beat, hammered out on tin cans and drums made from goat skin, is uninterrupted; it changes many times, is overlaid with different rhythms, but never stops: twenty different songs made into one long plaint. After two hours, we retreat to the Batwa sector of the village but the singers and dancers and drummers carry on, oblivious to the rivers of sweat that course over their bodies.

Back in their own village, the Batwa fling themselves on their mats and begin chatting. Their excited speech sounds like birdsong, a stream of bubbling, cackling, popping and purring. Now they are relaxed. They are overjoyed that we have come to stay in their half of the village, not in the Muntu half. Several of the elders have quite good Swahili and so we sit around the fire, warming our feet and laughing in the dark about the Muntu 'sultan' sulking below.

The Batwa have their own chief, and under stars so vivid they form a mist across the night, they give me a sociology lesson, though it is more like a comedy sketch, for they find everything funny, especially their own customs. One man sits up to narrate; the others lie on the ground, rolling around on woven mats; a woman kneads a man's feet. It is a matriarchal society but in a roundabout way: the next chief of the Batwa will be the son of the current chief's sister or, if no son is forthcoming, the husband of the sister's daughter. This, apparently, is hilarious. Women make all the decisions in the home.

'All the decisions?' I ask.

'Yes!' In the dark, the men and women laugh for what feels like half an hour. Sound lasts longer in the night, bouncing off the trees that surround the clearing.

A grilled chicken arrives, in honour of our visit, and the conversation turns to spirits. Colin Turnbull's famous 1961 book, *The Forest People*, tells of a spirit world that is very real to the Batwa, of the spirits that live alongside these people and the forest, the all-giving, supreme, spirit. Initially, the Batwa are reluctant to talk and descend into a fit of giggling at my questions, like embarrassed schoolchildren. They pretend that they have stopped believing in the spirits.

'So now you all go to church?'

'Of course, a man goes to church but when he gets inside his own house, it is a very different story', and they all laugh again. They explain how they take the bits of Christian tradition that they like, the bits that make life easier, and leave the rest.

'Before, if someone died, you'd have to pay a goat or a chicken or money. Now, there are no more death duties – you just go to the funeral in the church and it's finished!'

They sound like they're going to make themselves ill with laughing, the eruption crashing through the night, so present it sounds as though the spirits in the trees around us are laughing, too. As Turnbull observed, every feature of the landscape has a protective spirit, which, to continue its protective work, must be paid in beads or maize or blood. With some time, the Batwa acknowledge that the spirit world is very much alive. They know precisely where all the spirits live.

I point to a tree: 'is there one there?'

'Yes.'

I point again: 'there?'

'Yes.'

When the Belgians came at the turn of the twentieth century, they made themselves busy building railways and building mines but the Batwa continued to live in the way they had always done, almost undisturbed, according to a highly-evolved, symbiotic system, in harmony with the forest. During the second half of the century, however, their way of life and their forest were transformed by forces beyond their control. The Batwa don't know the value of money, let alone what value others may find in their land, their culture, their spirits and the riches of their forest, including minerals. They don't want to tell me any more.

'We found the coltan at Kisengo and now we cannot mine it. The Muntus always benefit, not us. We cannot give away the secrets of our ancestors as well.'

According to the few who remain around the fire, all now completely horizontal and happily looking up at the powdered dust of stars, the coltan at Kisengo was discovered by a Batwa named Kalegelege. Kalegelege used a very hard black stone to sharpen his tools. He became famous among the Batwa for it. The son of the local Muntu chief heard about this stone and asked to see it. The chief's son stole the stone and took it away from Kisengo, to Kalemie, where he confirmed that the stone was coltan. He made Kalegelege show him where the stone could be found and the Kisengo coltan rush began.

The Batwa have been denied access to the mine ever since.

At first, they cried foul. But the Muntu chief told Kalegelege, 'Who are you to get rich?' So Kalegelege left. This, the people circling the fire do not find funny, and the group goes quiet.

What has happened, and is indeed still happening, to the Batwa is a human rights catastrophe. All the more since the Batwa are the original Congolese. Yet talking about Batwa human rights in Congo is considered revolutionary.

The Batwa lose interest in Georges and me and murmur to themselves and stare at the stars. I ask Georges how he got into this line of work. Given the prejudice that seems almost universal towards these poor people, it is remarkable that he ended up with a different view.

'You know, Ben, I had fields of maize and beans, over ten acres', he begins, 'I worked in a bank, too, before the war. I was a man of means'. He says this as though he is not such a man anymore and it is a source of some regret. 'But then, the war, of course: the war destroyed everything.'

The Batwa are laughing among themselves, in great, brutal, hacking grunts, a sound that should come from a wild animal eight times their size, not from these friendly people.

Georges's face is pained in the firelight. He says: 'During the war I was idle. It is not a good thing to be without work'.

That is how he started camps for feeding the fighters in the bush. He thought if they could be enticed out of the forest then maybe he could reason with them. Others, including the US government and the World Food Programme, thought he had a good idea and gave Georges supplies to take into the bush.

'That's how I met my friends.'

The Batwa were the first to come into the camps. Perhaps the most hungry, they also had less to fear, since they were not wedded to any cause and had been conscripted by all sides in the conflict. Whoever was fighting, the Batwa were always thrown on to the frontline. Through them, Georges eventually made contact with the Mai Mai fighters, the freelance militias that wreaked such havoc in the lawlessness unleashed with the war.

'Slowly by slowly the word spread that they could get food and clothes. You know, life in the bush is hard.'

Once the Mai Mai started arriving at Georges's camps to collect their hot meals and clothes, he invited the UN to come and offer them demobilisation packages. The deal was they would get money and farming implements and other things if they agreed to lay down their weapons. And, amazingly, one by one, they did. It is no wonder everybody here loves Georges: he could be credited with a major part in bringing the war in Katanga to an early end.

War is about change. Changing a border, or a ruling power. But war can bring change in other ways, too. Faced with the truth about the Batwa, many people would have looked away. For Georges, the war erased old ideas.

'Knowledge eats at you, you know? My wife thought I was crazy at first. She said, "Why do you want to kill yourself for those people?" I was getting threats. But now she is the strongest defender of minority rights; my children, too. I have convinced them all, slowly. It wasn't easy but doing good never is, is it? I cannot do anything else now. This is my life.'

17

'Inhuman'

Mining coltan at Kisengo

I WAKE TO THE vraa-vraa-vraa of motorbike engines revving and tearing through the trees. Perhaps 'wake' is not quite the right word, since I don't think I really slept. Batwa beds are bamboo platforms, five feet long and several feet off the ground. Every toss and turn knocked my bed against the wall, causing dried mud to rain from the ceiling. I walk outside to find Tintin and Tonton engaged in their morning ritual of revving their bikes according to the ancient African myth: 'we have to warm the engines'.

Walking along the sandy road to Kisengo are men: Muntu, no Batwa. The men are off to the mines and we are going with them. They wear wellington boots and carry plastic buckets and bundles from which crowbars protrude like needles from balls of wool. This is the coltan miner's tool kit. It is as though the past century of industrial mining never happened and we are witnessing a first rush for minerals, apart from the plastic of the buckets, of course.

The road rises and falls, overshadowed by some of the tallest trees I've ever seen, and I've seen many very tall trees in Congo. This is old forest. Our motorbikes clatter through, showing no respect. Now and then, when the bikes gurgle across rivers, we stick our feet high in the air to keep them dry, and the engines cough on the water returning down the exhaust.

At the top of a particularly steep and muddy hill, the road ends in a forest of sticks. It looks as though a hurricane has blown through this town deep in the interior and stripped the huts of everything that was not nailed down or buried in the ground. The forest of sticks is the bare frames of what were once grass huts, row upon row. This is, or was, Antiochia, the grass city, where cholera struck two weeks ago and drove the inhabitants away as fast as any marauding militia or wind.

Antiochia was a brand-new settlement, the place where the extra souls who could not find a place in the mining town of Kisengo made their temporary home. Between Antiochia and Kisengo, the road is lined with small wooden crosses and mounds of earth. The mounds come in all sizes, from one foot to six feet. I count: there are ninety-six. Not the two hundred cholera victims claimed by the French NGO workers but precious lives, all the same.

The town vanished as quickly as it had been built. Many of the residents tried to go to Kisengo but the authorities, ever the entrepreneurs, realizing that a crisis can always be turned to profit, charged a tax to enter the town. Immediately, a barrier appeared on the road: twenty dollars for a car, five dollars for a motorcycle and one dollar a head for pedestrians. The barrier is still there, choked with people coming and going with goods for sale in this boom town. We stop in the clearing below soaring hardwoods; we have arrived at the mine.

Digging in the mine started only six months ago but already the village of Kisengo, made entirely from sticks and grass, has become a city of over twenty thousand people. Street after street of grass huts thread through the forest. The roar of generators has replaced the hum of rainforest; at the river, the relentless thuds of digging obliterate the babble of running water.

Despite the temporary town, the streets are named. One is called 'Avenue Force', another is 'Don't Lose Hope Street'. Some of the huts are the houses of miners; some are bars, restaurants, clothes stores, hairdressers. A Coke costs two dollars, a beer, four. A large woman, with perfectly coiled and piled hair and a spotless new dress, smiles when we complain at the cost of a drink. '*C'ést ça, la mine*', she laughs.

Prices are high because the town is awash with money. Brand-new, expensive American sportswear and designer clothes hang for sale outside grass huts. Well-dressed men, off-duty miners, saunter down the street. The people of Kisengo eat well too. In the rest of Congo, fresh meat is often hard to come by. In Kisengo, sides of goat hang in the main street. The smell of grilling is impossible to escape.

Columbite-tantalite ore – coltan for short – is used in the manufacture of the capacitors found in most electronic goods. Eighty per cent of known world supplies are found in the sandy riverbeds of eastern Congo, often in seams that also carry gold and amethyst. Coltan comes out of the ground as hard black granules or, if you're lucky, in larger hard black rocks. One kilo of ore is worth twelve dollars at the entrance of the mine, fifteen dollars to the traders in Kisengo, twenty dollars at the exchange in Kalemie but the world market price has remained at around one hundred dollars a kilo in recent years. The poor Congolese are, as ever, at the bottom of the food chain.

The value of money is relative; for the economy of eastern Congo, coltan is still a boon. Where farming or foraging is the principal means of finding food, mining coltan offers richer rewards, at a price. I follow Georges down to a maze of streams and huge holes in the sandy forest at the edge of the town. It is like an enormous badger set. Piles of unearthed soil stand among the trees. I narrowly miss stepping into one of the holes when a yelp rises from around the level of my feet. The yelp introduces himself as Shaaban.

'This riverbed isn't so good', complains Shaaban. 'Before the good spots were exhausted, I used to make one hundred, two hundred dollars a day. Here, I only find about twenty-five dollars' worth of stone a day and half of that I have to give to the soldiers.'

Still, miners can make more in one day than soldiers earn in a month. 'If you have a good day, they come and find you in the evening', says Shabaan. This may be a risky way to earn a living but it is a risk that he and many others are glad to take.

The coltan rush at Kisengo was so rapid that the local authorities recently issued an order closing the mine. Two months later, the mine is still officially closed but, bizarrely, production is going up. The closure has allowed the soldiers to control the mine and to tax the miners. Once again in Congo, it is the gun, not the law, which rules.

The system here is just like the mine at Bisiye run by Colonel Ibrahim and Sammy. Kisengo is one of the biggest informal mines in the east. The representative of the chief with responsibility for the mine, Mr Kabezya, has been side-lined; when Georges and I visit him in his office, he is angry. 'It's terrible, the soldiers have taken over our mine. They come here with dubious orders from their generals and then they fight among themselves.'

This morning, the navy and the infantry exchanged shots at six am. One of the navy boys had taken the woman of an infantry man. Kabezya is incredulous: 'What is the navy doing here? We are two thousand miles from the sea!'

Later, when we visit the police chief, he looks nervously out of his straw office at a rag-tag bunch of boys in fatigues carrying an array of rifles and one mounted belt-fed machine gun.

'Which ones are those?' he asks his deputy nervously, in Swahili. 'Are they the ones from Kongolo?' Kisengo is so over-run with armed men that keeping tabs on them all is impossible.

The police chief only has six officers in the town to keep a check on the two hundred heavily armed soldiers and their mine labourers. Each soldier controls one to five holes and each hole is mined by three or four people. Before the closure, there were more than ten thousand miners in Kisengo. The same number remains, still mining as before, except now they are subservient to the soldiers. Like Shabaan, they give the military half of their ore.

The real losers in the coltan trade are, of course, the Batwa. In the low grass hut, slightly bigger than the others, that is Kabezya's office, Georges confronts Kabezya with the allegation he has heard that the chief has forbidden Batwa from mining. This is the main purpose of our mission here.

'It is our custom', Kabezya explains, his voice rising, 'if a pygmy or a woman enters the mine, the coltan will disappear. Everyone believes that. I had no need to issue an order'.

He continues in the vein of the Muntu chief in the Muntu half of Kabala, 'If I am your older brother and then you become rich and you have money, will you still respect me? Of course not.' Georges doesn't press the point. According to Kabezya and his advisers, the Batwa are not indigenous to Kisengo anyway; the Kalanga people are. We give up, shake hands, and leave the men set in their ways.

Wryly, Georges says: '*Mficha uchi hazai.*' He who hides his nakedness will not give birth. We tried.

We decide instead to try to find the place where Kalegelege, the Batwa discoverer of the area's coltan, lives; a nearby village called Manowa. Driving away from Kisengo, we pass a group of men cooking by the side of the road, and a caravan of about five or six families, carrying possessions piled on their heads and heading towards the mine. I ask them if they are refugees.

'No, we are going to find life', says the woman in the lead, confidently. It is a proper gold rush. For some, the war has opened windows of opportunity. For others, like the Batwa, it has slammed them shut.

We think we know we are at Manowa when the gauge on Tonton's bike shows we have travelled seven kilometres. In rural Congo, directions come by odometer: 'it is at seven kilometres from the Kongolo junction' or 'it is at one-eight-four on the road from Kalemie to Nyunzu'. So we stop at a cluster of scrappy huts and ask for guidance to Manowa. No one will answer us. They merely point us to their chief, who is standing outside his hut in sunglasses, tracksuit pants and an Eminem sweatshirt.

'Is this seven?'

'No, this is six. What do you want to go to seven for? The Batwa lie anyway, there is no need to talk to them', he assures us.

A kilometre further on, at the next clump of mud huts, we ask for Kalegelege. The village is a dusty open space littered with mats and wooden furniture. A man appears in a white singlet and long trousers; his flip-flops are new. He holds a comb in his left hand and shakes our hands with his right. His name is Marco, and he is Kalegelege's cousin.

'We haven't seen Kalegelege for several months.'

All the people here came out of the bush recently. They say the chief at Kisengo threatened any Batwa found in the bush, so they settled in Manowa, next to a Kalanga village. But, after he had found the coltan, Kalegelege was afraid, so he decided to risk going back to the bush.

'It may be better for him there', says Marco.

At Manowa, they are bitter about the mining prohibition. The Muntu allow them to do construction work, and to sell things to the miners, but they are not allowed to touch the stones. They have grown terrified of touching anything that might be precious.

'If you dig, they beat you and put you in jail', Marco says. That happened to one of their friends from Manowa last week. 'If you are a pygmy the law does not apply to you.'

Here, the anger is more palpable than in the other places we have visited. Marco joined the army during the second war to fight for his country against invading Rwanda but now he is treated as though he is not a citizen. The Muntu call the Batwa monkeys and stop their children from going to school.

'They say a pygmy should not own a bicycle, because we are not human.'

Marco believes in God, and he says that if God has decided this life for the Batwa, then he must accept it. But sometimes his character will not allow him.

'I have put a sign on the door of my hut. It says "Inhuman"', he chuckles. 'Most of the time we can keep a sense of humour but sometimes I think it might be better to just get rid of all of us. If they do not want us to live like people, then let the president just round us all up, put us in trucks and drown us in Lake Tanganyika.'

18

The guns of Moba

The cathedral at Moba, on the eastern tip of the 'Triangle of death'

I STAND ONCE AGAIN on the quay at the port in Kalemie, waiting to board a southbound boat, contemplating the water and all that happened in the forest over the last few days. The day is clear and the lake has adopted the turquoise tinge of the helmets of the UN troops who are offloading another group of returning refugees from Tanzania.

Amid the chaos of mattresses, children and loading cement, a man strolls up and down the dock, carrying the carcass of a smoked animal by its hind legs. He claims it's a goat but it looks very small. The head is missing so it's hard to tell, but I am starving and need food for the journey, so I buy a leg, which the man hacks off with a makeshift knife and wraps in newspaper. It's probably a dog.

Watching on the quay beside me is a UN guy and it is from him that I first hear the phrase 'Triangle of Death'. Always eager to gather as much intelligence as possible, I am the annoyingly chatty traveller engaging everyone in conversation. When I tell him where I am heading, he frowns.

South of Kalemie, between Moba and Manono, he tells me, the country saw some of the war's worst fighting. Village after village was laid waste, first by the invading Rwandans, then by the Congolese forces pushing them out and, finally, the marauding, purposeless, Mai Mai. Towns changed hands many times. The Mai Mai are rumoured still to be active in the Triangle of Death. Manono, he explains, is the northern tip of the triangle, and Moba, the southernmost town on the Congolese side of Lake Tanganyika, its eastern point. Another town, Pweto, on the southern border with Zambia, sits at the bottom, forming a rough equilateral shape. My planned journey, from Moba to Pweto to Manono, almost exactly traces the triangle.

Fantastic. But I'm so close; I'm not going to give up now. I've heard scare stories before, only to find people wonderful and welcoming.

Of course, there is no information about the state of the roads or who might be travelling on them. All anyone in Kalemie can tell me is how to get to Moba: by boat. And so I board the MV Africa, a rattling old steel barrel of a ship from the Belgian days, with a dose of trepidation, a short nun, a man with a briefcase and an awful lot of cement.

It feels good to be on the lake again. Despite its status as a relic, the MV Africa moves quite fast, for Congo. By the time the boat leaves port the sun is throwing the shadows of the derricks across the lake, all the way to Tanzania. Soon, they are gone and the dark snatches Kalemie behind us. I sit on the deck and watch the glow of a large fire, far away and, further down the coast, the consistent prick of one electric light. Over in the east, on the Tanzanian side, the moon is shining bright, making a soup of the mist that hangs thick above the water. People are huddled across the deck, chatting and cooking, bedding down and the clanking of the diesel engine dominates the night.

As we chug past the low hills, I wonder about the fate of the peace that lies fragile and delicate over this land, like a spider's web. Several thousand square kilometres of Congo, from the Zambian border to Haute Katanga, including Manono, are silent, unreported. The security situation is unknown. For over a year, there have been hardly any news reports from here.

I paid for a berth on the boat and am glad of it. Although my tin can of a cabin is baking hot, in the middle of the night a promised rain finally breaks and everyone on deck scurries into the prow to take shelter under one tarpaulin. The boat pitches with the desperation of a fish on a line. Every few seconds a bolt of lightning flashes in the small square window of my cabin, keeping me awake and turning the cabin into a photo booth.

In the sodden grey blanket of morning, the jagged mountains of Moba come into sight. The settlement around the port is shabby. Rows and rows of pirogues are pulled just far enough above the waterline to escape the breakers that crash on the beach. The sea is riddled with rain. Our rusty little boat is strapped to another that is moored to the wooden quay; we must traverse it to reach dry land.

Unloading from one pitching boat is hard enough, doing it twice is not straightforward at all. Boxes, bicycles, photocopiers, birds, plants, cement, the nun, the business-man, twenty-nine refugees, the other passengers and me are passed above retching waves and below driving rain from one boat to the next and then across and on to the quay. Despite everything and everyone always being within the clutch of many hands, one photocopier threatens to make a break for the freedom of the deep. The old nun bal-ances on the handrail in her black slippers, grips a man's hand, and leaps.

Moba, too, is a town of two halves. By the lake and the port, the streets are close, grubby, and hot. On the hill above, a cool breeze comes off the plateau and blows down wide boulevards lined with ancient trees. The grandest street on the hill ends in an impeccably swept red mud road, flanked on both sides by huge palm trees that lead towards a twenty-foot-high wooden door: the west entrance to Moba's cathedral. Red bricks have been arranged and shaped with considerable care to create buttresses, flutes and turrets, a gothic masterpiece that would command stunning views of the lake, if only the grimy clouds would leave.

The UN staffer in Kalemie told me that eighty per cent of the refugees who fled to Zambia came from Moba district: the Mai Mai and the Rwandans cleared the bush of inhabitants and the town pretty much emptied itself as news from the countryside filtered in. The only people who stayed throughout were the priest and the nuns who run the mission, and that is where I go to seek a bed.

At the mission, I find the abbé, the Reverend Dieudonné, a large man in a cardigan and open sandals. He doesn't have any rooms but he invites me to tea in the vestry of the cathedral and explains that the mission and the church were constructed in 1883. It was the first Christian mission in the east of Congo, built because Moba was on the slave route from Mpala in the south to Karema on the Tanzanian shore. The missionaries were accompanied by a French mercenary, Captain Joubert, responsible for protecting them from the Zanzibari slavers.

Outside, beyond the mission's garden, are half a dozen abandoned tractors that cause Dieudonné to shake his head. The military took many of the church's vehicles; what he wishes for now, above all else, is a car, because he has not visited some of his parishes in the interior for years. But he is proud of the fact that he has never missed a service in Moba and on Sundays his church fills with over a thousand people. Dieudonné's main problem, at the moment, is a shortage of new recruits. He frets about the next generation of priests, while in the convent next door, there is no such drought among the nuns.

Through a little green door in a red wall is a court-yard, in which a bent, shrivelled nun sweeps the mud beneath three gnarled fruit trees: a guava, an orange and an avocado. Along one wall fists of roses are exploding in white. She looks up as I drop the latch on the door. 'I have rheumatism but I just can't abide rubbish', she says in French, by way of a greeting.

The ground is speckled with white rose petals and their scent clings to the heavy air. Finally, the sun breaks through and for a moment I believe I have slipped into a secret, parallel universe, as though the sun shines here alone in Moba.

Sitting on the veranda in a low wooden chair, wrapped up in a white blanket, is another very old nun; her skin is nut-brown and her hair bright white. She watches the comings and goings in the convent courtyard through slightly milky blue eyes. Her name is Gabrielle.

'My grandfather was Joubert', she says. 'I am mzungu like you'.

Her Swahili is excellent, unlike the usual pidgin Swahili of eastern Congo, perhaps learned from earlier generations of slavers from the coast. I learn that the French mercenary married a local Tabwa woman, Gabrielle's grandmother. When I ask her about the war, she replies, 'Which war?' and lets loose a cackle. 'Moba has seen many.'

As the Triangle of Death emptied of its inhabitants, Gabrielle fed thousands in this courtyard. She politely told the soldiers to remain at the gate and then brought them food, too. She is fascinated by my trip to find Manono and wishes me luck on my 'very long journey', before I disappear back to the broken muddy reality on the other side of the little green door.

I'm not a religious person. I have nothing but scepticism for the doctrines of the Christian churches but, in practical terms, Gabrielle, her sister nuns and Abbé Dieudonné are the only force holding Moba together. The mission fed and sheltered the area's inhabitants when they needed it and it provides comfort by the simple fact of its endurance, through all. Whatever happens to Congo, in one hundred years, I am confident that there will still be an elderly woman in white in a courtyard here, caring for the fruit trees, sweeping, feeding, singing and perhaps putting the pieces back together once again.

19

My name is Zongwe

Wartime graffiti on the walls of a burned-out home, Pepa

AFTER A LONG WAIT in Moba, I find a lift to Pweto in an NGO car heading west. The road climbs past the office of the territorial administrator, a 1950s concrete disaster on a bluff overlooking the lake; during my visit there earlier in the week, the resident administrator took refuge on his desk together with all his files, desperate to avoid the water pouring in great long strings from the cracks in the roof.

The road climbs to a plateau, where the gnarled trees are so black with wet they look like they have been burned. Every two or three kilometres, another village crumbles by the roadside. In one or two of the villages, the distinctive blue tarps of the UN have been lashed over rudimentary huts in the dome-like style of the local Tabwa people. The roofs steam in the rain as cooking fires smoke on damp wood inside and the people struggle once more to squeeze a living from the land that, several years ago, they abandoned in fear.

We stop for lunch at Pepa, the site of an old Belgian commercial farm. Beautiful rolling jade hills stretch in every direction: perfect cattle country. The herd here used to number sixty thousand and the farm employed hundreds of people. There is one employee left, Maurice, who looks after the remaining two hundred cows. It is a wonder there are any at all.

Towering pine trees scratch each other like animals shifting in a stockade and give the place a quiet, eerie murmur. Electricity pylons stand incongruous and abandoned, draping their wires, forlorn and forgotten puppets. Half a dozen white villas are blackened by fire, with glassless windows and waterless taps. Bizarrely, someone has trimmed the box hedges that fringe these wrecked houses; thus framed, they become almost exhibition pieces. A bathtub is upturned in the middle of a kitchen. Pipes hang

through ceilings, the floors are charred. There is no bro-
chure for this macabre museum. Instead, the nasty history
of Pepa is written inside.

The walls are a vivid riot of graffiti left by successive
occupying forces. No wall is blank, as if the soldiers were
starved of a surface on which to express themselves during
their months in the bush. Hundreds of tiny stick figures do
unspeakable things to other tiny human shapes. They carry
knives, sticks, machetes, guns, bazookas, bottles. They
stand alone, in groups, drawn one on top of the other, over
and over again. There are aeroplanes, helicopters, boats
and bicycles; forests, rivers, bullets, corpses. And words.
Lists of names, battalions and battles in French, Swahili,
English and other languages that I cannot identify, as well
as threats, insults and tag names shout at the empty rooms.
The largest name of all is scrawled along the top of a wall,
above a blackened window with a lovely view of the pine
trees: COMMANDER NINJA FORCE, CNF. I shudder to think
what the people of Pepa must have endured at the hands
of the men responsible for this torrent of terror.

Surrounded by rolling grassland, on top of the highest hill for miles, with a clear view of the road from Moba
inland to the mining areas of southern Katanga, Pepa was a
highly strategic prize in the second Congo war. It changed
hands three times in 2000, during the intense fighting between Rwanda, Rwandan-backed RCD rebels and Kabila's
Congolese army. Once the Rwandans left in 2003, Mai Mai
occupied the town and continued the reign of terror. Almost
all the people fled south to Zambia.

Lunch is in the office of Pepa's only charity, a small
NGO affiliated to the guys who are giving me a lift. All of
us who have hitched a ride in the NGO car sit around a
table while the cook fusses and apologizes over the maize

and eggs that he has rustled up at very short notice. I ask him his name.

'My name is Zongwe, sir', he says before disappearing into the kitchen, hands full of plates. Something about his gentle manner and assiduous care for his guests draws me to the kitchen after lunch, and we sit together on the wall in the sunshine. Zongwe was born here in 1975, when the town was still a Belgian farming community, and his whole family worked for the whites, whom he says were cruel. The family were paid enough to eat but that was all. There was no money for Zongwe to pursue his dream of going to school and so he joined the farm as a cowhand. Every year he would take the cattle to market in Lubumbashi, a journey of a month through the bush. One year, on the final day of the return journey, as he neared home, he met a man from Pepa running down the road in a panic. The man said that Pepa had fallen to the RCD rebels and everyone had fled.

In the 1998–9 advance that heralded the beginning of the second war, the RCD in Katanga was accompanied by the Rwandan army proper: the army had come south on the lake, landed at Moba, and were aiming for Lubumbashi, the jewel of Congo's mining sector; a decisive target. Across Congo, sixty thousand rebel troops advanced on three fronts, heading for Lubumbashi, Mbandaka, in Equateur and the Mbuji-Mayi diamond mines in central Congo. Eight national armies and twelve armed groups were involved. While President Laurent Kabila raced around Africa trying to drum up support for a ceasefire, Zongwe's family was hiding in the bush.

For two days, Zongwe walked and walked, looking for his family, until he found them sheltering in a village far from Pepa. The RCD rebels were in control there, too. Zongwe was put to work as a porter, carrying ammunition, food and luggage for the soldiers.

'You walked for a day. When you got there and delivered the stuff, you just ran!'

Finally, he and his family ran away and returned to take their chances in Pepa. They found the RCD still in charge. Zongwe worked as a porter for the rebels until the day the government forces marched up the long road over the hills from Pweto. The fighting was fierce. That was when Zongwe's family decided to flee to Zambia. Far from home, in the refugee camp inside Zambia, Zongwe suffered. He became ill with malaria; doing nothing in the camp drove him mad, so he decided to leave the rest of his family and come home for the second time.

'You suffer everywhere', Zongwe says, 'but at least Pepa is home'.

The RCD finally left. But when they did, the Burundians came.

'They were even harsher than the RCD!'

Then it was the turn of the Mai Mai. The Mai Mai hadn't chased the invaders out but they had become used to the soldier's way of life in Congo; the life of preying on others. They killed people. They woke Zongwe's uncle in the middle of the night, took him down to the fields and shot him. They raped most of the women in Pepa.

'If they wanted something, they would come and find you.'

But you could also give the Mai Mai money and they would kill someone for you.

'You know what it is like, there is always talk in a village. But you don't kill each other. The Mai Mai did not know the value of a life. For them, life was cheap, sometimes as cheap as a beer', says Zongwe, pulling at the grass growing in the cracks in the wall.

Eventually, the chief and others in the village united and refused to work for the Mai Mai. The strike worked and the last of the Mai Mai pulled out of Pepa just before the 2006 elections. Deals were being done with the leaders and demobilisation programmes were luring the Mai Mai back to civilian life. They are still around but they have handed in their guns, which means they cannot steal any more; their income-generating tool – the rifle – is gone.

'There is bitterness here', Zongwe says slowly, staring out over the pines to the valley below. Less than half the population of Pepa has returned.

'You see how quiet it is? It used to be a busy place. There were over one hundred whites, too, Belgians, working on the farm.' He lifts his nose towards the burned-out villas on the top of the hill.

From where we sit we can see an empty cottage next door. It still has lace curtains on the window and, like a European farmhouse, sports little blue tiles in the kitchen. A chicken coop is torn and bare. The roof of the wood store has fallen in.

'I think the whites are still afraid, because they have not come back yet.' For the Belgians it wasn't home, in the end.

Zongwe, though, is content. There is usually enough food in Pepa and the UN peacekeepers have finally shown up. He is living in his home; his mother and sisters will return from Zambia soon.

'I am lucky, I have work cooking here.'

Sitting on the wall in the afternoon sunshine, the only thing that worries him today, he says, is whether I ate my fill at lunchtime. I ask him about his hopes for the future.

'Maybe a wife. Children. Yes, that would be nice.'

Zongwe is smiling but the war remains very close here. The terrible, senseless and unremitting history of Pepa is written so thickly on the walls one can almost touch it. As though the murderers left the room only minutes earlier and the voices in the pines still whisper fear.

20

The return, part II

A man reunites with his family after seven years living in
a refugee camp

THE FIRST TIME I meet Leya, she is crying uncontrollably.

We are in the staff room of Kala refugee camp primary school, in Zambia. The room also serves as the school library and the headmistress's office. The walls are lined with charts and scientific tables and a full-length illustration of the human body, with the parts all named in French. Six or seven teachers are sitting in a circle and the headmistress is behind her desk, hair swept back, glasses on the end of her nose, wide brown eyes peeking above them, surveying the room. The female teachers on either side of Leya are stroking her hands; she and another teacher, Rafael, are saying their goodbyes. Their applications to return to Congo have been accepted by the camp authorities. Leya is going home, to Pweto.

I arrived in Pweto, on the shore of Lake Mweru, the week before, just as the last of the light was leaking into the west, leaving the sky streaked with pink creamy clouds. A line of winking lights marked the eastern horizon; hanging above them was a black cloud, blacker than the lake. The lights on the Zambian side of the lake were the work of fishermen, who lure their catch to the surface with lanterns. Now that I am on the Zambian side of the water, the black clouds are daily blacker; the rainy season is threatening to break at any moment.

Pweto was awash with rumours about tens of thousands of refugees desperate to come home, pestering the UN to repatriate them, faster and faster, from the camps in Zambia. Did the refugees realise they were coming back to a disaster? Were they proud and keen to make a new start in Congo or was it all rumour and they would rather stay in Zambia? The true test of peace is whether those who fled freely choose to return. And so I wanted to ask the refugees themselves. I decided to make one last detour from my route to Manono, to pay the camps in Zambia a visit and come back to Pweto with a returning convoy, before the rains made the journey impossible. A week later, I am in Kala primary school, surrounded by weeping teachers.

'We have been a family', says the headmistress in explanation, although none is needed. Looking at the school, I am doubtful that anyone would want to leave. It is immaculate, well-stocked, ordered and disciplined and, after the over-burdened schools of Congo, it looks half-empty, though there are hundreds of students here.

The rest of Kala camp is in equally good shape. In the Zambian bush, a model town has been created, as if it had arrived in a box. Identical red brick houses are arranged on a symmetrical grid of red gravel roads, lined with concrete drainage ditches. Every so often, there is a hole in the grid; when a refugee family returns to Congo, their house is destroyed.

The repatriation process is still under way, so the camp is a fully-functioning city, with its share of small comforts. The children in the school look well-fed: the pot-bellies of malnutrition are rare. There are water taps at every junction, a well-equipped hospital, a thriving market, and a bar selling moonshine brewed on the premises. Not here the queues of hundreds in Pweto and Baraka, holding their yellow jerry cans and fighting over the proceeds of a dribbling pipe.

The headmistress shares my scepticism; she says she wants to stay in Zambia.

'Do you really think the war can be finished just like that?' she asks me.

However, Leya is persuaded. Her husband skipped out of the camp illegally and returned to Pweto several months ago. He sent word that all is well and she should bring their five children back.

The hardest part for Leya is giving up her job. The extra salary she gets from teaching at the school has allowed her to buy things she wouldn't have dreamed of back home, such as a bicycle. Most of all she enjoys the satisfaction of being a professional. She is not a trained teacher, she has no certificates, but that doesn't matter in the camp; as one of few who can read and write, she is needed. She hopes to find a teaching job of some kind back in Pweto.

With a sigh, she wipes her eyes with the back of her hand.

'No. Seven years is long enough', she says, 'only the oldest child knows his own country'.

When the air-conditioned Zambian coaches hired by UNHCR rumble out of Kala camp, the passengers rise to their feet and wave ecstatically out of the windows, crying, shouting, singing. Outside, in the thin early light, the Congolese refugees who are left behind beat drums and ululate as if they are at a wedding.

For the first hour or so, the passengers behind me keep up a steady rhythm of singing and clapping. After a second hour, Lake Mweru appears through the acacia trees. It is a hazy day and the grey lake and grey horizon merge into a grey wall; the division between water and sky is lost.

Three hours later, we reach the border; the bus has fallen silent. I ask Leya how she is feeling but she doesn't want to talk. I go back and sit with Rafael, who is beside himself with glee. The Zambian government representative gets out to meet his Congolese counterpart, while the UN guys stand to one side. There is much shaking of hands and a formal handover of papers, a long list of names, probably not as long as either government would like.

As the coach draws slowly and officially through the barrier to Congo, a slow growl like an empty stomach rolls around the bus before breaking into a full-throated cheer. A song starts up but peters out quickly as anxiety takes hold. On the lake, two creaking junks sit low in the water, listing at an angle, crammed full of people staring at the coach as it crawls along the shore.

Rafael's face is pressed close against the window; nose flattened, eyes wide, drinking in the first sight of his native country in eight years. I ask him how it feels to be coming home, expecting him to be half-sad about leaving his paid job in the refugee camp; as a teacher he had been one of the lucky ones.

'I am a Congoman!' he shouts, pulling his face away from the glass and gripping the back of the chair in front. 'How do you think I feel?'

He glares at me, widening his eyes before breaking into a grin and throwing back his head.

'*Je suis fier! Je suis fier! Je suis fier!*' I am proud. It is the unofficial, nationalist slogan of Joseph Kabila's presidential election campaign.

At the reception centre, the refugees eat a meal before collecting their rations: the familiar thirty-six kilos of maize and ten kilos of beans per adult, as well as machetes, buckets, tarps and seeds. In recent months, Kala camp has received three hundred new arrivals because some Congolese, seeing the 'golden goodbye' given to the returnees by the UN, have decided to try and get a piece of the charity action. Unfortunately for them, they have been placed at the end of the queue and their entrepreneurial cunning will probably make them prisoners in Zambia for the next two to three years.

I talk to several families while keeping an eye on Rafael, in the corner, eating. He eats for a full forty-five minutes, filling and re-filling his plate courtesy of the UN's all-you-can-eat buffet.

Leya and her children climb on to one of the smaller lorries that will tour the town and drop off the refugees and their belongings. I jump on for the ride. We drive through town like returning heroes: children race after the white, UN-emblazoned lorries, trying to spot their friends. Wherever we stop, dozens of people line up for hugs of greeting. The townspeople help haul the enormous piles of mattresses, buckets, cooking pans and sacks of maize that the refugees have brought with them. Leya also has the fruits of her teaching wages: her bicycle, and a full-length mirror, wrapped in rice sacks.

She is the last to be dropped off. The lorry stops on the road and the kids and I carry the possessions down a track that runs between small plots of red, rich, fertile earth, turned and planted with cassava. On a slightly raised bump of ground, with a view of the plain sweeping down to Zambia, two houses stand next to each other. Leya, balancing a bucket on her head, talks absently to herself.

'Is it here? Is it here? Really?'

The children race ahead and a woman comes out of the right-hand hut. She looks at the children, turns, sees Leya, and shrieks. She runs towards us, wailing and waving her arms, which she throws around Leya with such force I fear for her ribcage. The two women hold each other, crooning. Leya has the biggest smile I have yet seen on her round, gentle face. Her friend takes the bucket and they walk the final steps to the house together.

The children are cavorting, though the door and back out, again and again. Leya thought the house had been destroyed in the war. It had. But her husband and the neighbours rebuilt it before she returned with the children. The orange mud walls glow in the sun and the lawn is a rich palm-green; the children roll across it as though it is the first time they've seen grass in their lives.

'So?' I look at Leya.

She shakes her head slowly from side to side. I see her lip quivering. She puts her hand over her mouth and turns her face from mine but her eyes are blurry and her cheeks are slick. She picks up the smallest child and holds him close as she walks very slowly around and around her house.

21

The lake of snails

Sign at Moba: 'Danger! Unexploded ordnance has been found in the water north of the pier. Watch out!'

WHEN I RETURN TO Pweto from Zambia, I meet an intriguing Englishman, Darby. Darby lives in a white-washed villa surrounded by a bamboo fence, on a hill with commanding views over Lake Mweru. In his compound, dozens of mortars are piled up like firewood under a small wooden shelter; at the back, several Landcruisers lie in various states of repair and a mechanic hammers at a wheel. Darby invites me to stay at his home.

Darby is a large, supremely generous, foul-mouthed, former Royal Navy bomb disposal expert. He is also a fantastic chef. Within minutes, I am drinking beer while he is preparing bangers and mash with sausages he has made himself.

The Navy was Darby's salvation. His dad had been brought up roughly, in a children's home. When it came to being a parent himself, he drank and then beat Darby, often without any reason. On his sixteenth birthday, Darby's uncle forged his dad's signature and Darby ran away to the Navy. Darby has only one regret about not seeing his father again before he died: that he never got the chance to beat the crap out of him.

After he was demobbed, Darby found that kicking his heels in suburbia didn't suit him. His wife allowed him to quench his wanderlust on condition he earned lots of money and treated her to nice holidays twice a year. She is expecting a five-star safari in a few weeks' time.

De-mining is dangerous, and therefore lucrative, work. Darby works for the Mines Advisory Group in Katanga province, clearing guns, rocket-propelled grenades, land-mines, cluster bombs and anti-tank mines from up to three hundred sites a month 'The arms here came from every-where', he reports. He says he has recovered and destroyed weapons made in Russia, China, the US, the UK, most European countries and former Soviet republics.

When villagers find a shell among the cassava, they know who to call. Darby has earned their trust. He recently got a call from a village on the road to Moba on which the Rwandans had buried dozens of anti-tank mines. But much of the work is more prosaic. 'The Congolese love to hide their bombs in loos', says Darby. He spends most of his time pulling grenades and rifles out of pit latrines.

The other place where retreating forces dumped their surplus explosives was the lake. One day, after someone told him there seemed to be something on the bed of the lake, Darby put on his scuba gear and had a look under the pier at Moba. What he discovered there made him very nervous. Nestling off the end of the pier, just where all the incoming boats to Moba dock, was a large cache of ammunition and at least six anti-tank mines. He immediately posted a sign, strung red tape across the pier and told the authorities to forbid boats from docking.

'A heavily laden ship could go up, easy.'

The authorities took the sign down.

Closing the port at Moba would be economic suicide for the town. The local officials are still wrangling about who will pay for him to clean up the stuff. I tell him about my arrival the week before in the MV Africa, laden with cement, pitching in a storm.

'I wonder how close the hull came to the submerged pile of explosives that morning?' I say with a nervous laugh.

'Inches', he says, 'a couple of feet, at most'. He leaves it at that.

Darby is sympathetic to my plan to get to Mitwaba and then Manono. He travels around Katanga more than most, including winching his 4x4, one tree at a time, over the mountains to the provincial capital of Lubumbashi but even he has no idea of how to get to Mitwaba. With the logic of a military man, accustomed to starting at the top, he suggests I try the chief of Pweto.

When I mention to the chief that I am hoping to reach Manono, he looks at me uncomprehendingly. When I try Mitwaba, he raises his eyebrows at the name.

'*Mitwaba? Ça c'est le Congo profond, ça.*' Deep Congo.

He says there used to be a road to Mitwaba but you cannot be certain of anything these days. Unfortunately for me, he is more interested in his own problems; he wants me to shout at the UN on his behalf, because he thinks the repatriation process has been going too slowly. His town is empty and he wants it full again, as soon as possible.

'They should just chase them all home', he says.

I point out that the process is supposed to be voluntary; that when the refugees feel it's safe to come home, they come home. This gets his knuckles whitening on the arms of his throne.

'Is Pweto not safe? Look around you!'

The hut where we sit is newly built. The roof is freshly thatched. The chiefly throne is waxed; the skin of a small wild cat is pinned to the wall, in a further show of chiefly status. But it is the only building still standing in his compound. Much of Pweto is in ruins. None the less, the chief announces that Pweto is soon to be an international tourist destination, as though this seals the argument, and he recommends I should go to the lake and see the progress that is being made. He also extracts a promise from me to look into what he says is the unfair treatment of artisanal miners.

In the early morning, I walk beneath the jacaranda trees that line the road to the Zambian border and return to the lakeshore. There is a Christian mission, with cars parked in the driveway and singing from the school next door floating into the street. A beautiful flowered compound is besieged by supplicants grasping sheaves of papers, waiting for a government office to open.

The lakeshore has become one large building site. Bulldozers roar up and down, a generator thuds heavily amid some trees and everywhere there are men in yellow hard hats. Engineer Davide has received a phone call from the chief on his throne and is expecting me.

'Welcome!' he says, taking off his hard hat to reveal a damp bald head. It's just after nine in the morning and he's been hard at work for several hours.

'Time for a beer!'

We drink an ice-cold toast to *le développement* from plastic cups and he explains the project to me. A kilometre of trees along the shore of Lake Mweru are being uprooted and several tonnes of sand will be shipped in, to make up for Pweto's lack of a natural beach. The hotel is going to be 'five-star', 'international'. He grabs a tube of rolled-up plans and spreads them across the table. The hotel is being built in the shape of a snail on its side. 'Why?' I ask.

'For that, you will have to ask the owner', he says.

'And who is that?'

'His Excellency Ambassador Katumba. He is an adviser to the president.'

Indeed, the magazine *Africa Confidential* lists Katumba Mwanke as the most influential power broker in Congo's lucrative mining sector, the man who 'presides over most big business deals'.

The ambassador has set a trend in Pweto; animal-inspired designs have caught on. The chief who was so keen for me to visit the project is also having a house built, a little further along the shore, in the shape of a monkey on its back, all four paws in the air.

Davide walks me through the circular snail foundations. Under an awning are a speed boat and a pair of jet-skis, purchased from South Africa for the use of future guests. There are plans for a national park on the hill above Pweto, plans to import wild animals from Zambia to stock it. Davide is enthused by the project.

'In six months, here, you will see a miracle!' he proclaims.

'What they haven't reckoned on', Darby tells me later, 'is that Lake Mweru is chock-full of bilharzia. There'll be no tourists going anywhere near that lake'.

Bilharzia is a liver disease, caused by a parasitic worm that makes a temporary home in freshwater snails before it finds a human victim. Also called snail fever, bilharzia is second only to malaria among parasites in the world. The snail hotel is either the most unbelievable irony or Ambassador Katumba has a sharp sense of humour.

Behind the site, on a flat plain, rows and rows of brick houses are going up. The hard-hatted men are swarming all over here, too.

'What are those?' I ask Davide.' Homes for returning refugees?' I imagine some kind of charitable side-line to the hotel project.

'No. The ambassador is building modern homes for peasants', says Davide.

The peasants in question currently inhabit a village overlooking Lake Mweru. The village is in a picturesque spot, beside a waterfall, where, unfortunately for them, the ambassador has decided to build a personal residence. Davide whips out another architect's plan: in a lavish flourish, a glass bridge will cross the waterfall to the mansion's front door. And thus one hundred and fifty families will find themselves in a new suburb of Pweto.

'Now they are living in straw huts, here we are building them proper homes', says Davide. 'They are very happy.'

Unfortunately, my time in Pweto is short and I am unable to ask the villagers' opinions. It seems like the height of madness, building homes for people who already have them, when so many have been destroyed.

Katumba may also be indirectly responsible for the other newly homeless people of Pweto. There are miners under every tree, littering the town's streets. I must keep my promise to the chief and find out what happened to them.

The *Bureau de service d'encadrement de small-scale mining*, as the sign outside puts it, is a small, square building, a two-room affair, next to Pweto's only speed bump. One room is curtained off, clearly out of bounds; in the other is a pair of desks. Behind one desk, adorned with a row of samples of all the different rocks that are mined in Haute Katanga – copper, cobalt, gold – is a stern-looking young woman who makes me write my name and business in a tatty exercise book. At the other desk is a man with a pointy haircut and smart sports shoes, his legs atop the desk, slouching in his chair.

'What's up?' he asks.

'I heard some of the artisanal miners had a problem', I say.

'Problem? Five thousand of them were put out of work', he replies, incredulous.

The miners who used to work the copper mines near Pweto are casualties of the new-found peace. Security has brought larger-scale commercial operations and the end of the copper rush for the little guys. There is supposed to be a policy to engage the artisanal miners in the new ventures but in practice the Australian company that holds the mining concession prefers to hire seasoned staff from Zambia's copper belt (just across the border, due to a trick of a colonial pen), with experience of modern machinery. So now the mines are ringed with razor wire and all day long five thousand newly redundant, 'illegal', miners mooch about Pweto, sleeping under the trees.

For the tin miners of Bisiye, the coltan miners of Kisengo and the gold smugglers of Yungu, there is a lesson in what has happened to the artisanal miners of Pweto since the multi-nationals arrived. Peace and commercial mining may raise the tax take of the government and benefit the nation as a whole but many families in Pweto will go hungry in service to this greater good and most of the riches, as usual, will leave the country. In peace, as in war, there are winners and losers.

22

Eating the neighbours

Decommissioned Mai Mai child soldiers

THE REACTIONS I GET when I mention the name Mitwaba expose a general unease about the place. Everyone has heard of it and yet no one knows how to get there; all I can gather is that it's somewhere out west, up high, on the plateau. On the map, one large road runs from Manono to Lubumbashi via Mitwaba, and a tangle of smaller roads snakes three hundred miles and more east, down the mountains to Lake Mweru and Pweto. According to one report, these smaller roads are washed out, and have been for several years. According to another, the Mai Mai has taken charge of the plateau. In any case, the rains have begun in earnest now and trying to get anywhere is considered utter foolishness. But Darby's mechanic has found a man who says he can get me there.

Papy is cocksure, brash. He waves his cigarette as he talks. Dressed in a white singlet and flip-flops, he looks like an off-duty gangster, an impression accentuated by his habit of yelling at his wife and talking on his mobile phone throughout our simple, brief interview. Papy knows the way: he's travelled to Mitwaba recently, he says, and the road is fine. It's about two hundred kilometres and it'll take about eight hours. For the ride, he will charge me one hundred and sixty dollars, about twice as much as I would pay in another part of the country. I dislike this short man with his quick hands and too-ready smile but I'll just have to meet his price and trust him.

The next day, after ten hours cramped on the back of Papy's Chinese motorbike, with my rucksack strapped to the front handlebars, we are still climbing endlessly up and up into the mist of Haute Katanga, the very roof of Africa. Mitwaba is not only deep Congo but also high Congo. Hills stretch to the horizon and somewhere over there, amid a wash of blue and green, the rainfall masses into several great crashing waterfalls, which drop to the plains beyond and to Manono. This plateau is the source of the great Congo River.

The road from Pweto twists and turns, folding back on itself. Above are the verdant hills of the plateau; below, deep valleys scarred red with mud. At each fold of the road, a pile of rubble nestles in the overgrown bush; the remains of razed villages. Every sixth or seventh village has been partially rebuilt. The depleted populations gather under tarpaulins stretched over the ruined walls.

Children scream uncontrollably as Papy and I zoom past on the motorbike but the adults cast wary glances from the safety of their hooded doorways. It is less than a year since the fighting stalled in this area. People are still jumpy. They have seen fragile peace before, only to have it shatter at the slightest touch.

Mitwaba is a tantalizing three hundred kilometres from Manono. It is also at the centre of the Triangle of Death and one of the last places where the Mai Mai laid down their weapons. Having met the people who ran away, now I might have the chance to meet those who caused them to flee.

When the road finally reaches Mitwaba, it runs straight along the crest of a hill lined by giant eucalyptus trees, then passes through two settlements, in between which sits the UN base, garlanded with barbed wire and guarded by a battalion of Indian Sikh men sporting huge moustaches. The base and its guards separate the smaller settlement, where most of the demobilized Mai Mai live, from the larger one, higher up, which houses the civilians who don't trust them. The larger settlement is where the Congolese army keep their base, as far away as possible from their old foes, the Mai Mai. In the middle of the larger settlement stands the Catholic mission, where, finally, in the dark, we pull up to find the abbé eating his supper.

'Ecclésiast!' exclaims Papy.

'Papy! Welcome. It's been such a long time. I haven't seen you since before the war.'

They know each other. Only now, as he slides my dollar bills into his trousers, does Papy admit, with a sheepish grin, that he hasn't made the journey to Mitwaba for more than ten years. We share the priest's potatoes and smoked fish by candlelight. The room is decorated with dusty icons, portraits of former pontiffs and hundreds of volumes of Belgian ecclesiastical publications dating from the colonial period. Old leather armchairs slumber around the room. The ceiling has fallen in.

In the morning, I am woken by a gentle knock on the little wooden door of my room and an old man silently points me towards a low stone building. It is the bath house. Inside, a concrete tub is brimming with steaming water, the most amazing and unusual luxury in a village without a container larger than a bucket. Praise the Lord. The grace and kindness with which I am received continues to astonish.

When I emerge, the abbé has gone about his business and a strange-looking man is standing under the blooming frangipani tree. He shifts uneasily as I walk down the path towards him. He points his one good eye in my direction and raises a bushy eyebrow.

'Sasa?' he says, which means 'What now?'

His eyes are arresting, slightly cloudy from creeping cataracts, wide-set and constantly shifting, like his crippled leg. He drags one leg behind the other and shakes it with annoyance, as though it is an unruly child. His teeth stick out; the bottom ones to such an extent that his lips do not close properly. This afflicts him with a constant drool, which, I notice, has already left a moist patch on his 'Manchester United' t-shirt. His name is Prosper and he has, for some reason, made himself my guide.

I will stay here for a couple of days to allow my body to recover from the gruelling ride before I must mount another motorbike for the last three hundred kilometres to Manono. Prosper will show me around.

'The administrator is expecting you', he says.

In his wood-panelled office, the administrator has an electric bell to summon his visitors but no telephone.

As the local law, he frets about rising tensions and the price of justice. The war here is fresh, the memories recent and the calm uneasy. Someone was killed in the Mai Mai part of town the week before and the administrator has arrested a group of Mai Mai whom he is holding without charge. The civilians are braced for more trouble.

Part of the problem is that, when I visit, the most famous Mai Mai leader, Kyungu Mutanga Gideon, is on trial in Lubumbashi for crimes against humanity. Other Mai Mai leaders believe they will be next. Gideon, Gédéon in French, was later convicted, along with his wife Monga, the first woman ever to have been convicted of such crimes. Gideon was the one who gave the area its 'nickname', the Triangle of Death. After the Rwandans left in 2002, the Mai Mai were neither paid nor disarmed and they went on the rampage until Gideon finally surrendered to the government in 2006. During the worst times, up to 150,000 people were displaced from their homes in central Katanga. Many of the hundreds murdered were killed towards the end of the carnage, when Gideon feared that the first 'post-war' elections would bring order and justice of precisely the kind that he eventually faced.

Gideon and his wife converted to Christianity after the war, a common turn among war criminals in Africa. I wonder if, since being born again, he has assumed a more appropriate name in place of Gideon, the biblical destroyer. He may well feel that God is more forgiving and fair than his fellow humans, who in March 2009 sentenced him to death while FARDC soldiers convicted of similar crimes were given sentences of only a year in prison.

In Mitwaba, the authorities are not leaving the issue of reconciliation up to God. The administrator's response to the natural suspicion that exists between the Mai Mai and their victims is to force them to 'integrate', by which he means move Mai Mai into civilians' homes. And so, a poor family, in a tiny two-room house exploding with children, must move into one room to accommodate a former militiaman, who may have participated in the butchering of hundreds of innocent people, and who brings his whole family, too. Unsurprisingly, most non-Mai Mai families are unhappy about the policy.

We leave the office and I follow Prosper's shuffling along the road to the second settlement, to which the Mai Mai have been moved. We pass the remains of a miserable refugee camp among the dusty scrubland on the outskirts. This was where the Mai Mai was housed and fed last year, when they handed in their weapons in exchange for a dismal hut, four hundred dollars and, some of them believed, a promise of immunity from prosecution. Only a few tiny bedraggled grass huts remain now; most have been dismantled or have washed away.

On the steps of a more substantial, more permanent house, Prosper simply sits down. A man comes out wrapped in nothing but a sarong. His name is Chikusi, and he used to be a Mai Mai captain. He didn't like his grass hut.

'I am a civilian now; I live in this civilian house with another family. There is no problem.'

He is in his mid-thirties. He joined the Mai Mai because he had heard stories about atrocities committed by the Rwandans against Congolese civilians and he wanted to drive the Rwandans out of Congo.

'Did you ever fight the Rwandans?' I ask him.

'Once', he says sheepishly.

After four years of surviving in the bush, Gideon called the Mai Mai together and told them to go to Mitwaba; the war was ending. So Chikusi came here and collected his four hundred dollars. There is no money left and he does manual labour to feed his family.

'We are afraid of the list', he says. The list that has been drawn up by the court in Lubumbashi.

It is impossible to picture this nice, smiling, relaxed man, sitting in the sunshine with a child on his knee, doing any of the things the Mai Mai did: raping, murdering, razing villages, eating people. Why is he afraid? I ask Chikusi if there are things from the war he regrets.

'You want me to talk about that?' he laughs. His wife and his children laugh, too. Do they know what he did during that time?

'That's deep, that's difficult. It was war. When there's war you do things that are normal in war. But now it's peace, there's no need for that anymore.' And he rubs the head of his son while his wife laughs and smiles and winnows the rice with her hard and wrinkled hands.

Prosper knows everyone and everyone knows him. The kids trail after him singing songs, chanting his nickname, '*Chef* Katumbwi'. He never asks for anything but constantly smokes the cigarettes I offer. His devotion is complete, to the point where one evening he goes out in the rain for an hour and a half in search of a single bottle of Simba beer for me. So I don't ask any questions when he decides that I must meet Monsieur Martin.

I follow Prosper up to an old, crumbling Belgian villa next to the army camp, in the upper part of the town. Steel pipes rust in the garden, a curtain stitched from World Food Programme sacks hangs across the door and an enormous log rests in the middle of a parquet floor. It is the office and home of M. Martin, the Mitwaba representative of the *Agence national de renseignements*, the Congolese intelligence agency.

Martin has none of the money-making zeal of his colleagues in other towns. He is supremely hospitable, calling out to a woman in the back of the house to make tea for the visitors. Prosper settles into a corner, while Martin tells me his version of the Mai Mai creation myth.

According to him, the Mai Mai were born of a power struggle within the Katangan *Forces d'autodéfense populaire*, the FAP, the home guard authorized by the national government to help push out the Rwandans. All able-bodied males were required to 'wash', to become initiated with the mai – Swahili for water – that the local militia believed would protect them from bullets, giving them their name, the Mai Mai. He says the Mai Mai were more of an annoyance than a threat to the Rwandans, who retreated to the richer pickings of the Kivus after the peace agreement of 2002. Once the Rwandans had gone, Gideon emerged as the leader in central Katanga but he refused to disarm, moving instead into the bush, where he recruited more soldiers. Children, too. There, he and his militia were said to practice sorcery using human body parts as fetishes and to drink their victims' blood; they maintained control through terror.

'They had no objective', says Martin. 'It was just idiocy, craziness.'

Martin's task is to collect evidence of war crimes and to disarm the remaining fugitive bands. Across the floor of his office he has stacked enormous files full of hand-written documents covered in multiple stamps like bruises and, as he talks, he scurries from one to the other brandishing his evidence. These damp piles are the sharp end of justice in Congo, the evidence that the courts will use to prosecute the people who gave this area its name.

He says the demobilized Mai Mai stay in Mitwaba because they are afraid of going back to their former villages. They fear the vengeance of their former neighbours in the Triangle of Death. Once lawless, these Mai Mai now need the protection of the law.

Next, Prosper takes me to meet the man who runs the centre for child soldiers. He is awkward, suspicious, a touch pompous. We must perform an elaborate ritual of displaying letters of accreditation, after which he wants a copy of my passport.

'The children are vulnerable', he says. 'I am sure you understand.'

There are 183 boys and two girls at the centre. Most were made to fight with the Mai Mai but a few saw combat with the Congolese army.

The two boys he summons to speak to me are not in a good mood; tough kids, with ready mouths, seventeen years old. They seem to be having a good time at the centre, where they are learning carpentry, but it is a skill that has been allocated to them. They also get food and clothes but what they really want is cash and the ability to learn other subjects, of their own choosing.

'Why do the grown-up soldiers get four hundred dollars when they give up their weapons and we just get this shitty counselling? What is that, after all? I want to go to school', says one of the boys.

After three months in the carpentry 're-insertion' programme, they will be either on their own or reliant on their families. There is no secondary school in Mitwaba but there is a farming school at Mwema and a fishing school on Lake Mweru, at Dubie. The programmes are funded by UNICEF, which has also reunited the child soldiers with their families. It seems like a good set-up and I feel the kids should be pleased, but they are grumpy and cynical and sceptical of most things adults have to offer. The Mai Mai and the army were not the only ones to exploit them.

'And what do we get from you? You write our stories, take our pictures, raise money for the "poor child soldiers", then eat it yourself. We know what happens.'

I protest but they are unmoved. When I leave, the pompous man shows me a large, beautifully illustrated book about the war in Congo, with touching photos of former child soldiers.

'I took those!' he says.

A photographer came to Mitwaba; he wanted to take pictures of the kids but was forbidden by the UN. Uncowed, he showed the man at the centre how to use a camera and he took the photos. Later, the photographer paid for him to

travel to Cape Town, where he received the copy of the
book.

'Pretty cool, huh?' he says.

The former child soldiers aren't wrong. If they saw
the photos, the documentaries, the lavish dinners in expensive hotels held in their name, they would be even more
cynical. They know that the pity they evoke has cash value
and that in peace, as in war, they are vulnerable to exploitation, including by those paid to help them.

Prosper introduces me to two aid agencies, one French
and one German, operating in Mitwaba. The German NGO
is run by Lilian, a well-dressed woman from Cameroon.
She used to work in South Kivu alongside many agencies
and just as many journalists. When she came to Katanga
province, she was shocked both by the scale of the need
after the war and the fact that it remained so unreported.
Katanga was peaceful; the war in North and South Kivu
was grabbing the headlines and the lion's share of the
humanitarian aid.

'I have never seen suffering on the scale of Mitwaba',
she says. 'There are no houses, people are naked, there's
nothing to eat and it's cold!'

Her priorities are distributing food and treating
sexual violence.

'By the Mai Mai?' I ask.

'All sides.'

She shares with me the case of a woman who came to
the local human rights centre in Mitwaba. After being kept
by the Mai Mai as a slave in a cage in the bush for months,

she escaped and ran to the next town, where she was raped by the army. When the army left, the Mai Mai took over again and put her back in the cage. The woman had lost count of the number of times she had been raped.

I want to know what led apparently normal young men like the ones I have met to rape and kill and Lilian invites me to come and meet some of the families.

Early the next morning, we drive west on a rutted and treacherous track to a place called Mubidi, where Lilian is organizing a food-for-work programme. The sky darkens and cracks with rain. As we get closer to the village, more and more men pass us, pushing bicycles laden with huge blue and white sacks of maize, stamped 'World Food Programme'. They are heading not towards the village but in the opposite direction, back towards Mitwaba, on their way to sell Lilian's food rations at the market. The first there will get a good price, before the market is flooded. Lilian is exasperated.

'Do you know how much it cost us in petrol to ship this food?' she fumes.

She had to arrange for the roads to be improved and for bridges to be built and then she spent thousands of charity dollars on fuel for a fleet of small jeeps, since large trucks are too heavy for the local wooden bridges. She tried to get the villagers to participate in the road-building, because part of her mandate is that the local population should contribute in kind towards things that are for their benefit but they told her that the road was fine for their bicycles. If she needed a better road for her cars, she would have to build it. They didn't themselves expect to have cars any time soon.

'Sometimes I think we should just dump the maize in the market in Mitwaba and give them the money!' she laughs. Bitter laughter.

When we get to Mubidi, the food has long gone. A few crumpled nuggets of dried maize are trodden into the mud next to fresh bicycle tyre tracks.

While Lilian goes to shout at people, I sit in a small wooden hut, its grass roof teased by the wind. Micheline, a young woman who is helping Lilian's agency with the food, introduces me to Ngoy and his wife, who have agreed to speak to me. They are joined by three onlookers who cram into the hut and settle themselves along a tiny bench.

Ngoy has red eyes. He looks tired and the story he tells exhausts us both. He was here when the Congolese army came to fight the Rwandans in 2000; when the Rwandans left, the military stayed. He witnessed the Congolese soldiers behaving badly, saw them tie up men and rape their wives in front of them. When the FAP turned against the soldiers to protect the civilians and became the Mai Mai, they were popular. Ngoy was happy, too; everybody wanted the Congolese soldiers gone and Ngoy supported the Mai Mai when they chased the army to Mitwaba.

The problems started when the young men of the village came back. Ngoy grew worried when, he says, the Mai Mai returning from the front made demands: 'we've been fighting, what have you been doing? Bring me food, bring me firewood', they would say. For the first time in their lives, they were powerful and they liked it. If the Mai Mai wanted someone's daughter, they simply took her. They coerced men to join their ranks. Ngoy was old and so avoided conscription but the Mai Mai had no qualms about recruiting more children.

'They did things I cannot talk about. I am lucky I do not have a son. They bound my sister, hands and feet, they put firewood, petrol, and they set her on fire, and they sang their songs. Because her son would not go to join them and fight', says Ngoy.

The Mai Mai plumbed the depths of human depravity as they forced parents to give up children to their gang. In the paranoid fog of war, they felt they had been betrayed by those they sought to defend. They ate infants, burned parents, forced sons to kill their fathers and rape their mothers. Such horrors, once uncorked, are hard to tame. Gideon was in charge here then.

Ngoy ran away. The whole village ran away. And when Ngoy and his wife came back, they found every house had been levelled. No building remained standing, because the population had refused to help the Mai Mai fight. The villagers were refugees, finding shelter in the bush and in Mitwaba for six long years; only in 2006, after word spread the Mai Mai were demobilizing, did the villagers began to return and to rebuild.

'But as soon as they handed in their weapons they came back here, to the village', says Ngoy.

That is because, to a large extent, the Mai Mai are the children of the village – the children that were recruited by nationalist sentiment, bravado or force. Their parents live in Mubidi, their land is here and so is their best chance of food. They cannot return to live side by side with the people they terrorized, however; what they did is too unspeakable. People are still afraid, peace is delicate and this village is far from Mitwaba and the protection of the army. For their part, the Mai Mai fear revenge. They fear that the angry villagers will make them pay for the shameful crimes they committed. No one wants to have a former Mai Mai as a neighbour.

The people of Mubidi, and others across the Triangle of Death, have found an uneasy solution: villages rebuilt in two halves. Mubidi 1 and Mubidi 2. One village for those who were in the Mai Mai and another for their victims.

Ngoy continues talking while his wife holds his hand. She listens, staring out at the rain, her eyes focused not on the rivulets running off the straw roof but on the lush green hills further away.

Their daughter was snatched by a Mai Mai soldier. She went off to the bush with the militia and now she has three kids. She and her children and the former Mai Mai live in the other village, Mubidi 2, but Ngoy will not speak to her. He will not set foot in her house, nor will she set foot in his.

'She is ashamed. She was taken by force', he says.

She sends messages with her children and Ngoy plays with them outside the house; they do not come in.

'They are afraid of their own family', says Ngoy, his eyes slowly brimming.

He looks at me quizzically, as though I might understand the tragedy of it all but then thinking better of it, he asks the question of his wife.

'How could she stand there while the man who is now her husband beat and humiliated her father? She can never face me now.' He still cannot understand how, the night she was kidnapped, his daughter did nothing to stop her future husband from beating him. He constantly re-lives that night in his mind and continues to feel that awful pain every time he sees his grandchildren innocently playing outside his house.

His wife, who has said nothing all afternoon, nods her head and squeezes his hands. She gives a gentle smile in a

practised manner, all the while staring out at the rain
coming down on the far-off hills.

On my final day in Mitwaba, in the bedraggled refugee
camp at the Mai Mai end of town, Prosper introduces me
to Benjamin, Gideon's father. He lives in one of the few
shelters that still stand. No one wants him in their house;
what would happen if his warlord son were to visit? The old
man must sit in his hut, six feet by four feet, with a ripped
plastic tarp over the top, alone, although the last time he
saw his son was a year before his trial.

Benjamin's face is drawn, his grey hair the colour of
dirty steel. His little tent is filled with so much stuff –
broken radios, cardboard boxes, bits of metal that have no
apparent purpose – that there's barely space for a bedroll.
There isn't room inside for the two of us, so we talk in the
drizzle. I ask him what Gideon was like as a boy.

'Oh, very smart, just like his mother', says Benjamin.
Before becoming a warlord, Gideon was a teacher and initially, by all accounts, he was a benevolent warlord.

Benjamin says he hasn't suffered any prejudice on
account of Gideon; the people of Mitwaba even give him
food when he can't make it to the aid distributions. Such
generosity surprises me. I ask him if he has heard what
Gideon has been convicted of – masterminding the killing
and raping of hundreds, if not thousands, throughout the
war – and he shrugs.

'I hear what they say. But that's for the court to decide.
I am proud of my son. A father must always be proud of his
son. Even though I don't know what the point of all that

fighting was.' His main complaint is that Gideon never sends him any money, as though that would make everything better.

When I contemplate Gideon's crimes, I try to imagine what might make a person act in this way; if there is some underlying trigger. How is a warlord made, really? Was it something in his upbringing, something nasty, deeply buried, that in the pressurised chaos of war was given oxygen and took fire? Benjamin appears to be a nice man, an ordinary dad. When he shrugs off the conviction and complains about the money Gideon should be sending, he is speaking as a displaced person and like all displaced people, he is usually hungry. Food is what Benjamin thinks about most of the time.

'You know what I'd really like?' he asks.

'Tell me.'

'A cigarette. It dulls the need for food.' He laughs. I give him all the cigarettes I have and we sit in silence on little blocks of wood outside his tent, smoking in the rain.

23

Of pigs, rabbits,
and popes

Soldiers of the *Forces armées de la République Démocratique
du Congo* (FARDC)

IT IS MY LAST evening in Mitwaba. Tomorrow I will follow the road that runs along the crest of the hill, out beyond the army camp to the north. The road is no longer a road, they say, but it's passable on foot. It takes four or five days to walk to Manono; one, or maybe two, on a motorbike, if you are lucky enough to find one. I am lucky. I have found one; or rather, Prosper has found me a man that has one.

As we return from meeting Benjamin, the rain retreats and the sun appears briefly in the thick clouds and casts its long shadows through the eucalyptus trees before disappearing over the rim of the world. The whole village seems to be enjoying the sunset. Men, women and children are taking an evening stroll, engaging in conversation, carrying loads, the last work of the day. No one pays any attention to a pig, bound with rope on the steel rack of a bicycle, howling like a child being dragged off to school. The caterwauling is unbearable. I don't understand why I am the only one wincing at this noise that breaks the calm.

From the direction of the army camp comes a line of police and soldiers, which advances down the centre of the road with the heavy footfall of the drunken. When he reaches me, the commanding officer salutes with a mangled arm. One soldier lags slightly behind, more drunk than the rest, stumbling a little, shoving his rifle up his shoulder now and again to prevent it falling. The police and soldiers laugh at the pig, then pass on. The man pushing the pig-bearing bicycle remonstrates with the lagging soldier but the soldier waves him away; he doesn't want to know.

The man hands the bike to a passer-by and follows the soldier down the street. From behind, he slips the strap of the rifle from the soldier's shoulder and returns to the bike with the gun. By the time the soldier has realised his loss and retraced his unsober steps, the man has cocked the weapon, put it to the pig's head, and pulled the trigger.

Perhaps the pig was going to die anyway, perhaps the war has changed the conditions of reference for the use of force, or maybe the pig's transporter was just pissed off.

The wiles of Congo are difficult to understand, especially for those who might wish to help its citizens. The other aid agency in Mitwaba, the French one, is run by an Americanized Frenchman, Julien, who has invited me to my final supper in town. When I arrive, he is angry because he has just discovered that his satellite connection is down again. His satellite dish is the only means of accessing the Internet in the village, and he allows others to use it, but it frequently crashes, he says, when the Sikh soldiers from the UN base are downloading too much porn.

Julien's other preoccupation, one of his projects in Mitwaba, is rabbits. He keeps abandoning our dinner to rush out and tend to the two hundred rabbits that arrived today. The idea, cooked up in Paris or Kinshasa, is that the people of Mitwaba will breed rabbits to sell and eat. Rather like Yvette and Bienvenue's project to give goats to the villages on the shore of Lake Tanganyika, Julien will hand out free rabbits to get Mitwaba started. And like the goats, there is a problem.

Rabbits won't eat any old grass; the plain grass of the plateau is too tough. Earlier, Julien had to send motorbikes down to the river to get bamboo shoots for them. He is worried that the villagers won't take the time to search for appropriate food for the rabbits when they barely have enough food for themselves and, in the absence of afford-able maize, bamboo shoots have become a local staple. I suspect his anxiety is well-placed; in the contest between humans and rabbits for the bamboo, I have little doubt which will triumph. Mitwaba's happy residents will be eating meat again very soon.

It is not just the foreign NGOs whose well-intentioned efforts often collide with the local particularities of this vast and varied country. When I was in Moba, the governor of Katanga province turned up in his private jet to exhort the population to 'develop'. He commandeered all the vehicles in town for his motorcade and kept the residents waiting in the street for two hours in the hot sun. The shade of the bus shelter, built for the buses that will grace Moba's streets some day in the future, was reserved for VIPs: foreign staff from the NGOs.

In his speech, the governor announced that he had brought two hundred bags of cement for rebuilding schools and, as a finale, roared: 'I heard you were suffering from a lack of an ambulance in Moba, so I have brought one!' Right on cue, a white four-wheel drive, a red cross painted on its side and a red light mounted on its top, drove through the crowd with every light flashing madly. The people cheered.

'What's more, this ambulance is modern, it has plastic inside', shouted the governor. More cheers.

Later, in the hospital, Dr Kiwele laughed. 'The gov-ernor brings an ambulance but what we need in the clinic is drugs.'

As the governor had demonstrated, getting a car is not the issue. In an emergency one can usually be found.

'I would have told him what we needed. All he had to do was ask.'

After dinner, back at the venerable collapsing Belgian mission, it's a big night. Father Jean has guests. They have come to share two half-litre bottles of Simba beer, brought all the way from Lubumbashi, along the terrible road that in the rainy season becomes impassable. Soon, as the rains fall harder and the trucks stop coming, the supplies will dry up and there will be no more beer.

We drink from very small glasses. Jean pours some of the precious amber liquid for me; three pairs of eyes sadly watch the level in the brown bottle subside.

It is a special occasion, so the usual candles have been replaced with a single electric bulb. The sound of a generator labouring to power it chugs from the courtyard. The portraits of the popes high on the wall are illuminated for once. I had assumed that the television sharing the shelf with a row of church magazines – the entire back catalogue from 1929 to 1958 – was just for decoration but it actually works and is showing an absurd bolingo video. The turbo-charged Congolese guitar screams at top volume and lifts the priests' spirits.

For reasons that remain a mystery to me, dwarves find ready work as dancers in the music videos of two African countries: Nigeria and Congo. In this video, dwarves are vigorously throwing their hips from side to side in the garden of some cheap hotel in Kinshasa. Their dance is intercut with stolen footage of the Parisian skyline.

The five of us – four middle-aged priests and me – hold beer glasses aloft and attempt to gyrate in similar fashion beneath the beatific gaze of the pontiffs of the twentieth century.

I am sure they would approve.

24

La route principale

Erité on a bridge over a tributary of the Kalumenamugongo river

THERE IS NOT MUCH left of *la route principale*, the main road linking Lubumbashi with the Belgians' largest tin mine at Manono. Benjamin Péret, a French author writing at about the time this road was built said, '*La Nature devoré le progress et le dépasse*'– Nature will always devour and surpass progress. Nature has indeed reclaimed it now. Manono no longer boasts the largest tin mine and the road is no longer a road, more a footpath.

On its journey through the centre of Mitwaba, along the ridge lined with eucalyptus trees, the road is for a moment grand and wide but on the edge of town it peters out. For three hundred kilometres, the sun, the rain and the irrepressible bush have attacked the Belgian colonists' engineering triumph like a tropical virus, eating it inch by inch. There is not a morsel of tarmac left. All that remains is a path that is by turns swamp, boulders, meadow or sand.

According to Prosper, the only man in Mitwaba with a motorbike capable of making the trip is Erité, and Erité is unsure how long it will take: he has only done it in the dry season.

Erité is a man on the make, with a kind, hospitable streak that he struggles to hide under a thick skin of bravado. I am in his hands for the final leg to Manono. He shows up dressed in a shiny silver waterproof jacket and smelling of alcohol. 'It's cold', is his surly excuse. It is also raining; not good. Mitwaba is high up in Haute Katanga, on what is called the Upemba plateau, and the dawn reeks of damp.

As soon as the road leaves the town in the mists of the forest, the rain breaks and the hills steam in the morning sunlight. The path falls from the ridge after we pass a garage, reduced to rubble, the cars it used to service long

gone, and then what used to be the Mitwaba general hospital, also in ruins. A huge red cross hangs hopefully on the
hospital's rusty gates; beyond, a frangipani tree grows inside
the building, its chubby twigs fingering the few remaining
roof tiles.

Lower down the hill, as the forest gives way to the
narrow flood plain, is a group of collapsed houses, a former
sanatorium for tuberculosis patients set up by the Belgians
to keep sufferers away from the rest of the population.
Most of the houses are smashed to pieces but some have
been patched up with plastic sheeting or mud, to make the
shells habitable by a few families. For the many refugees
roaming Katanga, a reclaimed ruin beats a bivouac of
branches and UN plastic.

In the early light, the valley is beautiful. The river
brims after the rain, carving a rich brown swathe through
little greening squares of cultivation stitched across the
valley floor. The gently rolling hills look like whales, breach-
ing. The clouds are bunched in retreat, sullen and jealous
of this delicious burst of sun.

We clatter over the river on a brand-new steel bridge,
built by the UN in an attempt to wrest the road from the
clutches of the bush. Erité turns his head and shouts into
the wind 'The name of the river is Kalumenamugongo. It
means "strong man" in Kiluba'. The river curls in on itself
like a sleeping snake, squeezed into its narrow bed.

All along the sides of the valley are mounds of bright
white stones, débris thrown out by the diggers of the informal tin mines. The hill on the other side is steep. In several
places I walk while Erité pushes the bike over steps of rock
and around boulders. Along the path we overtake legions
of bicycles laden with enormous one-hundred kilo sacks,
pushed by men slick with sweat. To reach the outside world,

the tin ore from these white hills must creep along this road on the back of bicycles. This road that once, when it was intact, carried hundreds of lorries, buses and trucks. The men with the bicycles are paid fifty dollars to spend four days pushing one hundred kilos over three hundred kilometres. Erité's is the only motorbike making the trip and in the dry season it takes him one day to carry twice as much, a tidy business.

The men pushing the bicycles shout and laugh at him and he laughs back. 'They want my motorbike', he says and smiles. I'm not surprised. We have to lift the bike up a two-foot-high stone step. How the others manage with one hundred kilos of tin on the back I have no idea.

At the top of the hill, the straggly scrub turns to soft grassland flecked with orchids and primroses. This is Lac Upemba National Park, the catchment area for the Congo River, and the mists and showers that envelop this spot feed a steady flow of streams that eventually cascade down an escarpment into the swamp from which the great river emerges, slow, fat and brown. Here and there the plateau cracks into deep valleys, choked with forest, and the track we're travelling cracks too. The hard mud is broken by huge red rocks and turns downwards at terrifying angles; it looks more like a riverbed than a road. When it rains, it probably is one. Then the track disappears, zigzagging into the forest down the escarpment, and Erité skids to an abrupt stop.

I ease myself off the back of the bike and gingerly test my legs for the first time in several hours but the view forces me to sit straight back down. The land sweeps down before us in a tidal wave of foliage as the plateau drops away on either side. The sense of an endless sea is uncanny. In the middle distance, cerulean in the midday sun, a succession of minor hills spill towards the swamp. Somewhere out there in that swamp, the Congo River begins its long journey to the Atlantic.

Erité points to a narrow path that descends precipitously through the forest. 'Follow that path. You will arrive in Ntambo in thirty minutes. I will meet you there.' The road is too rough for a passenger.

'What if I get lost? How will you find me?'

'Don't fear, you won't', he reassures me and before I can argue further, he is gone, bouncing off over the boulders, twisting the bike this way and that.

In an instant, the trees gather me in their humid embrace and I am folded into another world. One minute I am perched on a rocky outcrop looking at what feels like the edge of existence and the next I am in the humming forest, surrounded by clouds of butterflies. There are wild orange trees and enormous mushrooms; rubber trees smoothly ooze their lucrative sap; parrots and go-away birds shriek and click in the branches above. The path carries me over massive roots and through thick undergrowth, where, with each rustle of branches, I am showered in seeds and bombarded with indescribable fruit.

The forest is a fertile ball of energy, a pot simmering on the stove, ready at any moment to erupt and take over meagre human advances. If people did not constantly cut it down and keep it in check, the forest would colonize all their projects in a couple of brief seasons, just as it has reclaimed *la route principale*. My path emerges at the bottom of the steep wooded valley and opens on to a spectacular view of many more valleys disappearing into the mists.

Eventually the ground levels out and I come into the village by the back door, through small vegetable gardens and between huts, until I hit the main track. Here, it is a broad avenue lined with ancient mango trees, another legacy of Belgian planting. I must be a strange sight, a white man in a t-shirt, with no bags, walking into town like a spirit from the bush.

Ntambo is a settlement of bicycle mechanics. In decades past, the town serviced automobiles and now it attends to the bicycle trade. Livelihoods depend on the ingenuity of these mechanics to make the Chinese bikes fit for a job they were never designed to do. The country runs on these cheap imports; without them, the trade along this road would be reduced to what people could carry by hand. Porters squat under the trees among discarded peel and rotting mangoes, eating the fruit and the fried yams cooked in smoking oily pans by village girls. Crowded and noisy and thick with the smell of cooking, the town has the feel of a rural wedding party.

The chief of the bicycle mechanics is a curious-looking man, wearing a purple ski jacket. The nail of his little finger is distractingly long; one of the big toenails emerging from his sandals is painted purple, in a fit of co-ordination. His hair is dyed black but the roots are grey. He hustles me inside his dank hut and seats me on a plastic jerry can as onlookers join us.

Ntambo was founded in 1935, when the Belgians first needed to build the road. They ordered the people living in the forest nearby to move down to the valley, so they could work on the construction. But no one today is willing to say a bad word about the Belgians, for the road has been their lifeline. In the bush, nothing happens and life is hard, but the presence of a road means that rare thing; that people pass by, and spend money.

The escarpment up to the plateau above Ntambo is steep, so the Belgians only built a single-track carriageway.

There was a gate with a bell at Ntambo, and another at the top of the hill. When a car came down the hill, the bell would be rung and it was Eugène's job to close the gate and make ascending cars wait; when a car was ready to go up, he would ring the bell and everything happened the other way round. Eugène is the oldest man in the village and as he tells the story, he smiles. 'Those were good days.'

The road brought the war to Ntambo too. The first the residents heard of trouble was from the streams of Hutu refugees on the road, fleeing the attacks on the Goma refugee camps in 1996. They took four days to pass. Since that initial flood of thousands, every military group has passed along this road. Ntambo is a strategic site, from which the army could guard the high plateau of Katanga and its mineral riches from the rebel strongholds in the east. Three times, the villagers were forced to run away and survive in the bush on what they could find. Each time they came back, the military put them to work. When I ask why they didn't just stay in the bush, the old men smile at my naiveté.

'Have you tried eating berries and roots? It does not take long before bellies start to swell and faces go blue or pale. Some people went as white as you!'

The last time the Congolese government made any repairs to the road at Ntambo was in 1982. Twenty-five years is all it has taken for nature to reclaim it. The track may be in a bad way but it is still a godsend: it brings bicycles, pedestrians and trade. Without those, the people of Ntambo would be even more hungry. The UN is re-building the road bit by bit and like their grandfathers, the villagers are finding work as labourers. But it is slow going. I ask why it is taking so long, and get a round of chuckles in response.

'Do you want us to finish it all at once? Then how will we eat?'

I stoop out of the shadowy hut into the illuminated afternoon to find Erité sitting under a tree calmly smoking a cigarette. A torn leaf at his side holds two pieces of fried yam.

'Have a yam. It is still far, no?'

He and the chief embrace and chat excitedly; they know each other. Erité finishes the remaining half of the yam and we make our departure.

Bouncing away from Ntambo, Erité shouts over his shoulder, 'Is this a road? This is not a road'.

After a short time, we cross a bridge in the forest over a ravine fringed with daring acacia trees clinging to the sheer sides. We haven't travelled very far but Erité pulls up for a rest. We smoke a cigarette looking down at the river through branches laid sideways on the steel girders. Thirty feet below, the brown river churns between the vertical walls of the gorge. The sunlight, dappled through the clouds, covers the hills in regulation camouflage.

'That chief. I used to live with him. He knew my father. After they killed my mum …' A pause. We watch the river.

Erité's father was a ranger, as was the chief, in the Lac Upemba National Park; their families lived in the rangers' homes there. When Gideon's Mai Mai moved into the park, they came to Erité's house. His dad was not there, neither was he. The Mai Mai took his mother and his two sisters away with them; his younger sister was just ten.

They killed his mother after she became ill and refused to walk any more but his sisters were with the Mai Mai for nine months before they escaped, with another woman, and reached the village of Genga. They are safe now. Erité fled to Lubumbashi where he learned mechanics, borrowed money to start his business, and bought the Yamaha.

'It's a good bike, huh?' he asks.

'Yes.'

I don't know what to say. Murder and rape were so widespread that no one is unaffected; no one's story is remarkable. These horrors have become almost casual, an experience worn as lightly as possible. Everyone is simply an individual in the here and now and no one asks too many questions about where you might have been; war is the ultimate leveller.

'But I will buy a bigger one, an even better one', he says.

He gives a smirk, as though laughing at himself, and climbs back into his skin of bold *machismo*, which cloaks the pain and tenderness within. He returns to his cigarette and the view of the churning brown river that roars below us.

Erité seems happier. Is happier. Every piece of the past that is remembered, mourned and released leaves you lighter. He opens up the Yamaha and the mango trees race by.

Descending into a patch of bamboo forest, just before Kinsha village, we pass a man and a young boy standing on a plastic sheet by the side of the road. They are naked to the waist, their chests glistening with oil. Next to them, a plastic bucket and a bundle tied with a kanga, the Swahilis' cotton sarong, sit on the ground. The man and the boy are going to Kinsha, after being away for five years. They have walked for five days from Mitwaba, taking the same road as us. A woman wrapped in another kanga, carrying a baby on her back, comes up a small track from the stream, where she has been washing. It is a Steinbeck moment, another wandering family in a country set adrift on tides of hunger and war. They are putting on their good clothes before entering the village, because they want to look their best for the homecoming.

'It's a special day!' says the grinning man.

When we get to Kinsha, there is business to be done. We pull up by a low concrete building with POLICE painted in faded lettering on the outside. Two very old men in very faded light blue uniforms, who look as though they have been policemen since the 1950s, sit on stools under a home-made thatch shade. They say hello lazily, smile, and resume their silent watch over the road. Erité talks to a friend, a shifty-looking man wearing a long, once-beige jacket, whose deep pockets bulge with something mysterious. He pulls out his fists and unfolds a paper bag. Gold. He runs a gang of miners in which Erité has invested; they dig the gold and Erité sells it in Lubumbashi.

The normal price of a gram in Kinsha is four thousand francs, about eight dollars, but Erité gives them only half of that, because he has bought their equipment and subsidizes their digging expeditions. In Lubumbashi, he sells the dust for twenty dollars a gram, a hefty mark up. I admire his entrepreneurial spirit even as I disagree with his miserly rates for the diggers, especially since the gold is found in a hot spring and getting at it is a scalding business.

We speed through a village where women are clearing away the little tables from which they sell goods by the roadside. Voices ring through the mango trees, calling children home. To the east the sky is black and palm trees bend in the wind. The thunder sounds like a steel ball swirling around an oil drum; flowers fly off a frangipani tree like a burst of blizzard. A few drops of rain speckle the sand.

We drive on under the blackening heavens. 'We will make it to the next village', says Erité confidently. We don't. With a crack and a tear the sky falls. We cannot see a thing. Erité struggles bravely on but the bike plummets with a thump and disappears into two feet of water. Instantly, the road has become a river. We heave the bike out and proceed cautiously, the wind ripping at our sodden clothes and the rain stinging our flesh. We are lucky; a kilometre on, a village appears.

The inhabitants of the first house we see laugh at us but make space on the porch and bring chairs. Three men sit in a row staring at the rain while in the doorway a young mother, no more than sixteen, breastfeeds a child and contemplates the grey wall that has enclosed the village with a deafening hiss. It is like being trapped inside a television that picks up no signal. I watch the sky flicker and think for a moment that no one but these people on the porch knows where I am. I take out biscuits and pass them round. Everyone pulls out biscuits, passes the packet along and eats, saying nothing, a hushed communion. Erité offers damp cigarettes and we smoke, watching and listening to the rain.

We won't make Manono tonight. We decide instead to try and break our journey at Mukanga. Martin, the ANR intelligence man in Mitwaba, told me that Gideon is from there. But Mukanga is in the middle of the swamps and the road ahead is probably under water. We push on in the failing light, through village after village, along watery tracks, until the path simply ends in a muddy cliff and our old friend, the Kalumenamugongo River, now flowing quickly and at least fifty metres across, five times wider than when we last met a hundred and fifty kilometres ago, blocks our path.

There never was a bridge here but there was once a concrete slipway where now there is only the raw red mud of the riverbank. Four steel canoes, slung together with steel girders welded across their tops, serve as a barge. Two chains at either end are attached to a cable that traverses the river like a high wire. The boatman pulls these chains to tilt the barge so it catches the current, which pushes the craft and its passengers across. It is ingenious as well as free, operated by a cheery man in a grey suit jacket and red bandanna with a cigarette delicately balanced on his bottom lip.

When we eventually reach Mukanga, the hills we have left behind are turning purple in the dusk, topped by pink clouds that reflect the sunset from the west. Here in the swamp the air is heavy, the bell-like domed skies of the plateau and its sharp clear atmosphere a memory.

We get lost in the wide darkening boulevards of the once great, now half-empty, Mukanga. Arranged on a huge grid are scores of similar roads bearing little steel name-plates in neat blue lettering that has worn to a dull sheen. The buildings are large, made of brick, with tall windows and great, square doors, as though Frank Lloyd Wright had paid a visit between the wars. Every second or third house is an empty shell but from the others the weak smoky light of oil lamps sneaks through cracked windows and half-boarded shutters. Grass covers half the boulevards and the snaky patterns of bicycle tyres and feet weave through the mud. Cars, if there are any left, don't frequent these roads. The heavy rhythmic pulsing of bullfrogs fills the air. We see no one.

The chief, when we find him, dismisses his other visitors and receives us, a forlorn bedraggled pair, on his verandah. He sits to one side in his leather jacket and smart trainers, regarding us with a quizzical air.

'I think the first priority is to find you a room, and then, after that, maybe a bath?' he says in French. I couldn't agree more.

Erité pulls off his wellington boots and pours about a pint of water out of each one, then, with slow heavy movements, stuffs his bare feet back in them. The chief organises a room while his assistant, Fidel, a nervous man with thick glasses and a check shirt, stares at us in wonder.

'What on earth brings you to Mukanga?' he wants to know.

'The rain. And Gideon.'

Gideon is, in part, a product of Mukanga's inaccessibility; the town is surrounded on three sides by rivers and lakes. The only road is the one we travelled. Contact with the other towns in the marshes is mostly by boat; the capital of the district, Malemba-Nkulu, is five hours away by pirogue. The water is both conduit and curse, since the river brings, along with scant people and supplies, every upstream epidemic to spread throughout the marsh.

'Mukanga is no better than a sewer', says Fidel. 'The Belgians did nothing here; they did not leave even a bridge.'

While they complain of it, their relative isolation is something in which the people of Mukanga seem to take pride. It has shaped their attitude to the rest of the country for generations. Even when, courtesy of Belgian mercenaries and the pro-Western leadership of the politician Moise Tshombe, Katanga seceded from Congo on 11 July 1960, a month after the country gained independence, the people of the marshes resisted a government that was closer to them than Kinshasa. The disinterest of Kinshasa suited them quite well. In 1964 the young people rose, in a group called *Mouvement de jeunesse*, joining with Antoine Gizenga's Simba (Lion) rebellion, which spread across eastern Congo in support of the assassinated President Lumumba's ideals. The young rebels wanted socialism, not the government of cronies installed by Belgium to safeguard their mining interests after Lumumba was killed. Further north, Che Guevara and Laurent Kabila were also trying to join in. Che and Kabila were driven into Tanzania, however, and in northern Katanga the rebellion ended with Congolese government planes dropping bombs on the marsh villages.

Thirty years later, in 1996, Laurent Kabila's chance finally came in the shape of the uprising orchestrated by Rwanda. He found a ready audience: people were keen to help kick out Mobutu. They had had enough of the dictator. When the new government's troops started living off the population, just as their predecessors in Mobutu's army had done, the people initially supported new rebels, this time the Mai Mai militias. Once the government realized that it could not defeat the Mai Mai in the marshes, it began wooing their leader, Makabe Kalenga Ngwele, with money and gifts, and one of Makabe's commanders, Gideon, became jealous.

As the legend goes, Gideon said, 'Why should he get all that when he did not work to chase away the Rwandans. Makabe has never crossed the Congo River!'

A civil war among the Mai Mai factions followed, with Mukanga at the epicentre. The town was razed several times, as the Mai Mai became what they had vowed to destroy: raping, murderous parasites. Eventually, the residents captured Makabe's deputy, Kabale Makana a Nshimba, whom they shot and killed on the lake.

The trial of Gideon and his wife is a source of pride and anxiety to Fidel, who drums his hands on the rough wooden table as he talks. He doesn't quite believe that the state can keep the former warlord behind bars. (His fears were realized on 7 September 2011, when eight gunmen sprang Gideon from death row. Desperate to have him back in prison, Katangan authorities put up a $100,000 dollar reward for information leading to his capture.)

Mukanga seems to be another city conceived on an architect's drawing desk in Brussels, the product of the liberal colonisers' sentimental idealism. But Mukanga's wide boulevards and modern villas are no match for the town's enduring bad luck. Last year, the harvest was halved by flooding; earlier this year, just as planting began, elephants hunted by remnants of the Mai Mai living in the national park escaped and stampeded through several villages, destroying much of the crop.

The chief's son interrupts us and whispers in his father's ear.

'*Monsieur*, your bath is ready', says the chief curtly. With that, our conversation is ended.

In my damp, heavy clothes, I follow the boy over stepping stones down an alley between two houses. Light is showing beneath a wooden door. Inside this rough, modern, breezeblock building, candles surround a souvenir of the past: a deep porcelain bath filled with steaming water. A pumice stone and a natural sponge lie on a wooden stool on the concrete floor. After the soaking rain and the aches of the motorbike, I am very grateful. These kind people do not know us, yet have dropped everything to talk to us, warm us, feed us, house us.

After me, Erité has his turn, and then the chief's son takes us to the Hotel Sekas, the only functioning guest house in Mukanga. Following a woman holding a candle, we pick our way across the stepping stones in the courtyard; Mukanga's response to the floodwaters. A quilt of World Food Programme rice bags over the doorframe bestows some privacy; a leather sofa in the hall has been re-upholstered with others. Little blue-painted tin signs marked *réception* and *réfectoire* are nailed to the disintegrating brick.

I have an iron bed in room three. The ceiling has fallen in and the holes in the roof are mirrored by little puddles on the floor. The iron bed has a gingham bedspread; a matching scrap makes up a curtain. It looks cute, sort of European farmhouse *chic*, but underneath the blankets the mattress is wet and the sheets are full of dust. The whole room stinks of death; it cannot have been slept in for years but as soon as I am in that damp bed, I fall instantly asleep. It is the dreamiest bed in the world.

In the morning, the chief walks me around his town, down wide streets trimmed with green hedges, which give the whiff of an American suburb, post nuclear war. The chief is particularly proud of the airstrip, currently under water. We finish with a tour of the ruins of his house and the carcass of his Land Rover, both torched by the Mai Mai. He has written his memoirs to try and promote peace in the region. He shows me the manuscript, typed in French, entitled *Reflections from Over Thirty Years of Service of a Chief of a Sub-district in Katanga Province, Democratic Republic of Congo*.

We say our goodbyes and Erité and I strike out across the marshes, past huge papyrus plants and giant lilies and gladioli. My legs are like two wooden poles after the pounding of the day before.

'Only one hundred and fifty kilometres today!' Erité beams.

If it's anything like the last one hundred and fifty, it will be hell. This time, when we cross the Kalumenamugongo River, I chat with the boatman with the bandana. I am incredulous that something should be free in Congo, particularly something so useful. The *Office des routes* is responsible for maintaining the free barge, he explains. The *Office* sounds grand, conjuring an image of a large building in Kinshasa populated with many sharply-dressed people in sharply-pointed shoes with nothing much to do.

'But I have not been paid since 1990', the boatman reports. 'So the villagers usually give something when they cross, like a fish or soap.'

Possessing neither, I give him cash. Erité drives quickly and smokes cigarettes at the same time, the smell of alcohol coming over his neck and hitting me in the face. For hours and hours I close my eyes and cling on, willing us to arrive. At one point, we rush by a bombed-out truck with no wheels, pointing towards Manono. The retreating Rwandans must have abandoned it there. Eventually, the marsh dissolves into open water, a large lake, on the left, and the sky above turns black. Jungled hills loosen on our right and in the distance is a steel grey snake of a river.

'The Congo!' shouts Erité above the roar, thrilled. At this seminal moment I can only continue to close my eyes and continue to cling on. The horn screams under Erité's palm and the crowds of people carrying loads on their heads – baskets of fruit, bundles of firewood, roofing poles – scatter.

The next instant, palm trees appear and beyond a square-topped hill, white but at risk of going green where the grass creeps up its slopes. It is the tailings heap that I recognize from the photographs! The signature of the tin mine. We must be there. Finally. The bike pulls level with the hill and *la route principale*, which has run true for three hundred kilometres, ends in a crossroads. On either side are bombed-out buildings; in the middle is a metal sign that has seen brighter days: SOYEZ LE BIENVENUE À MANONO.

25

Beer and normality

Jean-Baptiste with his motorbike, amid old mine
machinery, Manono

MY ARRIVAL IN MANONO is unceremonious. I stand wet, filthy and bow-legged in front of an impeccably-dressed Congolese priest. My legs feel as though they are going to give way at any moment. The priest is Abbé Jean-Baptiste; he serves at Manono cathedral. He sets down the shoes that he had been polishing and goes to find the curate. There is a room, he reports. Dinner is at seven.

'You must be tired.' He looks kind. I sense immediately that I can trust this deliberate priest whose first question to me is whether I 'use' alcohol.

'Great, then perhaps after dinner we can go and taste a little beer', he says.

I say goodbye to Erité, whose waist I have gripped for three hundred sore kilometres. I will miss him and his shifting face, ragged beard, brown and bloodshot eyes; his quiet, quiet voice. I am finally here.

It is strangely appropriate that Erité has delivered me to the Catholic mission, a centre of calm and normality, of regular masses, meals and laundry amid Manono's turbulent history. The missions of Congo embody the resilience of everyday life, a daily slice of permanence. I am exhausted but elated. The little I have seen of the sorry, sodden town, muddy streets and crumbling buildings is very unprepossessing but to me it feels like walking down Fifth Avenue in Manhattan for the first time. Somewhere I have imagined so often yet never seen.

The low, red-brick mission building has an iron roof and smooth concrete floors. A young girl in a white shift winds a rag along the verandah, leaving the floor glistening with little number eights. There is solace in the right angles of the courtyard, the scrawny flowers in pools of red mud and the washing blowing lazily back and forth in the breeze. And in the knowledge that priests have been baptizing, marrying and burying people who came to make their living at this muddy spot by the river since tin was discovered here by an intrepid Belgian official in 1906. The mission has seen it all: the early days of industrial mining in the 1920s and 30s, the heyday of the post-war commodities boom, the 70s decline and eventual collapse. And then, of course, the war.

Over the decades, as the mountain of white tailings grew taller, the village of Manono became a city. Like many other new towns across the Belgian colony, *avant-garde* urban planners and architects were eager to apply their theories to Manono's virgin jungle, to demonstrate the power of architecture to bring white and black together, to inspire everyone to create a wealthy modern nation. The Swiss-born Le Corbusier was a strong influence on the young Belgian architects working between and after the world wars. These architects had Utopian ideas about urban space, believing, like Le Corbusier, who designed the UN building in New York, that through the shape of their buildings they could actually change the world.

The world, and especially the Catholic Church, habitually resists such ideas. The mission and the cathedral that tower above Manono are redolent of conservative tradition, a rebuke to the hopeful folly of the modernist planners and a reminder that feeding, clothing and caring for people is sometimes all that is possible. The huge cathedral, built in wood, slate and brick and topped with a gabled turret, would look completely at home in a provincial northern European town. Look here, it proclaims, it takes more than a few buildings to change the direction of a culture. After all, it took the Christians over one hundred years to sow their seed in Congo.

The avenue of eucalyptus trees that leads from the mission to the cathedral divides the city in two. Manono is not really one city: the Belgians built one town for the mostly expatriate mining staff and another for everyone else. The mission sits between the two, mediating like a referee, holding the balance between the colonizers and the colonized, between the European modernist dream of what Congo might be and the harsh African reality of what it is.

Dinner with the priests is a tense affair. They question me aggressively and are jealous that I appear to have been co-opted as Jean-Baptiste's guest. It is like sitting down with a bunch of bitchy schoolgirls. Not surprising, I suppose, since the mission is not unlike a small boarding school. The priests' rooms lie next to each other, they eat three meals a day together and there's only one bathroom.

We say grace around the heavy dark wood table; chicken stew arrives on stainless steel platters. The conversation is erudite, fast and informed, ranging from US foreign policy to football, God, the general election and the purpose of my visit.

'Wait for me outside', Jean-Baptiste whispers as the dishes are taken away. He wants to go for a beer after dinner but he doesn't want the others to come: 'it will be expensive for you', he explains. It turns out to be expensive anyway.

The rainy season has cleared the sky and the stars glint sharply – a fistful of diamonds scattered on velvet. One other priest, Abbé Simon, whom Jean-Baptiste couldn't shake, has come along for the ride. The three of us perch on Abbé Jean's motorbike as he steers through streets painted with muddy puddles to a house owned by a man named Robert.

On the way we pass a crumbling building bearing the legend *oxygene* in a block font across a concrete wall. Just visible inside, cylinders squatting like a store of ammunition, are hundreds of oxygen tanks, overgrown with grass and rusting, all that is left of Manono's pride and joy: its brewery. It is hard to believe that this ruin once supplied beer to the whole region. The local tipple was *Nyota*: 'star' in Swahili. The last bottle was drunk sometime in the 1980s, after the world tin price collapsed. Jean-Baptiste swears it was the sweetest-tasting beer on the planet but it is unlikely that Nyota will ever be drunk again.

No one has opened a bar in Manono since the war; beer is only just becoming reliably available once again, a sign that things are beginning to get back to normal. Most of the drinking happens in private homes, 'beer houses': Chez Bernadette, Chez Bonga, Chez Albert. Robert has built a small straw hut in the compound of his house and that's where the drinking happens tonight. We share the compound with about two hundred children sitting in the mud watching a television powered by a generator. The generator is so loud, I'm sure they can't hear a thing. Robert says he set it up for his kids and lets the others come for free.

'No one has any money anyway. And certainly not for beer, except the priests!'

At four dollars a bottle, I am not surprised.

Robert makes the journey from the hut across a series of bricks set into the puddles, returning balancing a tray bearing a tall brown bottle and three glasses. He wipes the glasses and the bottle and places them in front of me and my two hosts, Abbé Simon and Abbé Jean. Simon and Jean cannot take their eyes off the bottle, which is marked with a white stencil of a lion and, in the middle, the hallowed red word 'Simba'. His hand on the trademark light blue bottle cap, Robert looks up expectantly. Jean nods his head and, with a flourish, the top comes off. Jean pours the precious golden liquid into the three glasses, and we drink a toast. 'To the river.'

The revered bottle has travelled more than six hundred kilometres by barge, up the Congo River from the southern provincial capital of Lubumbashi. It's a two-week round trip to fetch it. Robert's wife is currently making the trek back with fresh supplies. She is expected tomorrow. Jean had promised me a tour of this town that I have sought for so long but at the mention of the barge he changes his mind.

'The barge! Now, there's a thing. You must see the port – it is a tourist attraction!' he announces. 'The town is there every day.'

I am in his hands, so that is where I'll be going tomorrow.

26

The bend in the river

On a rusting hulk, boys await the arrival of the barge, Manono

THE NEXT MORNING I am groggy and grumpy. I can't remember how many bottles of Simba we had but my plastic bag of Congolese francs seems much lighter than before. I have a dim memory of the three of us on the motorbike, wobbling home through the streets in the moonlight. Jean-Baptiste, however, is thrilled with his hangover, a badge of affluence. He grumbles loudly, theatrically clutching his brow and shaking his head as we pile into the truck to head to the port.

If you look at a map of Congo, it is dominated by the river. A vein steadily fed by more and more capillaries, the river starts as a tangle of thin tributaries in the far southeast of the country and grows thick as it makes its way in one huge curve towards the Atlantic coast, where it spills the rains of central Africa. Near the beginning of the arc, amid the spidery tributaries, before the river even officially has the name Congo, is a small bend, no more than a kink. That is the spot I spied in the map room in London, the place where Manono's people made their port.

In the early days of the Belgian colony, when roads did not exist and planes could not land in the jungle, the river defined the lives of those in what was labelled, in that mysterious way, 'the interior'. Today, in many parts of the country, the roads are unreliable, the railway a memory and the planes are only for the rich, so the river is once more the channel of contact with the rest of the country.

The large barges pushed by tugs, famous on the stretch from Kinshasa to Kisangani – that original town on the bend in the river of V. S. Naipaul's book – and upon which every famous foreigner from Joseph Conrad to Humphrey Bogart sailed, are not found upstream. The river here, above the rapids, is narrow and the traffic is light; the vessels are more like over-sized canal boats and just as unseaworthy. For a while, when the fighting was hot, these shallow-draught barges didn't sail, but they are finding their rhythm again.

Abbé Jean's truck doesn't have a starter motor. He sent money for a new one to a priest in Lubumbashi who pocketed the money, so instead we take four boys along in the back: they are the starter motor.

'You know, a starter motor is great, because then you can go anytime you like, even at night.'

Also along for the ride is Jean's older brother, known as '*grand-frère*'. He sports a nylon cowboy hat with the string pulled tight under his chin, slicing between two folds of flesh. He is plump these days but during the war he nearly perished from starvation.

'The people who knew me then, do not know me now', he says.

After forty minutes of racing along sandy tracks, the wide brown river comes into view. As a mark of solidarity, everything else has turned brown, too. The old rusting train tracks that snake through the grass and come to a halt by the water's edge just above the concrete jetty are brown; so are the broken rusting cranes that would once have lifted ingots of tin from the impatiently puffing trains on to a parade of waiting barges. In the mud, sailing on a thatch of grass, is the brown rusting hulk of a forgotten boat, deposited high and dry by a retreating flood. The sea is on the other side of the continent but a shell of a building, the victim of several rocket attacks, has *Bureau de maritime* scribbled in charcoal above the door. As I have found all across the former war zones of the east, bureaucracy has survived the war relatively unscathed: there really is an office inside. The officials within make more fuss about the weekly barge from Lubumbashi than their predecessors did over the daily cargoes of tonnes of tin despatched down the river in times gone by.

Tied to two enormous stakes driven into the mud bank is this week's vessel: a colourful, battered barge divided into two decks, with a heavy diesel engine in a cage at one end. Below, just inches above the waterline, cargo of all sorts is piled in boxes. Above, in a narrow deck just high enough for a toddler to stand upright, are the passengers. They travel lying down and must enter and exit on hands and knees. Some are disembarking, whilst others lie under their blankets, trying to ignore the tumult on the bank. The barge has another five hundred kilometres to go, to Kongolo, further downstream, where the river meets the railway. From there, an irregular train rattles north now and then but nobody knows when or how far it goes.

The first cargo to come off the barge is petrol, in large yellow jerry cans. The rest seems to follow in order of priority: beer, sugar, rice, Chinese batteries, powdered milk, juice, biscuits, then cans of Coke and Fanta. Waist-deep in the silty brown river, strong men lift sacks out and pass them, one man to the next, up to the bank. Nearby, a small boy casts a line tied to a rock strung on a bamboo pole into the river, apparently playing at fishing. But beside him is a small metal dish full of little quivering fish, so he must be doing something right.

About a hundred people sit and watch the unloading. We join the audience and eat small fish dabbed with black spots, which taste as though they've been fried in engine oil. Pirogues bring in enormous catfish, three to four feet long; four dollars for the biggest ones. There are children everywhere, under the wheels of the trucks, up the rusting cranes, wrapped around my feet.

When the unloading appears to be nearly finished, a huge white UN truck rolls up, and a mixture of Congolese and UN troops spills over the tailgate. The UN soldiers are in battledress, with bullet-proof vests and weapons at the ready. The Congolese soldiers, on the other hand, look as though their ragged uniforms won't last another week. The UN stand guard while the Congolese chat among themselves and shout orders to six men who are unloading a blue tin trunk secured with two giant padlocks: the army's salary for the month. Several other items make their way into the UN truck – a generator, a tape player, a goat, a bicycle tyre.

Cigarettes are a peculiar currency in Congo. All the little kids milling about the port carry empty cigarette packets tied to sticks with pieces of thread. One boy has a packet tied round his waist like a belt, proudly displaying it by tucking his shredded T-shirt into his shredded shorts, even though inside is nothing but a few cigarette butts. I ask the boy why he carries an empty box like that. 'To show people I have something', he says, matter-of-factly. To show people he is someone. He carries a broken sandal in one hand and on his head is a woman's lacy summer hat, the sort of thing that might have once been worn to a wedding. They pose for photos but their fun is interrupted when word comes that the pick-up is loaded and it's time to go.

The car is full of goods for *grand-frère*'s shop. This must be the real reason that Jean-Baptiste insisted we meet the barge. It seems a most unlikely tourist attraction; coming here has cost me fifty dollars in fuel. But that's how it is in Congo: he who can, pays and as many people as possible jump on for the ride.

Grand-frère is a canny man; he has rebuilt his life, his church (he's Lutheran, and a pastor) and his business in a few short years after all was swept away in the war. The day

gunfire came to Manono at dawn, the whole town emptied
into the bush. He walked for four days looking for his children, eventually finding a huddle of Manono refugees living
in the bush; the lactating mothers breastfeeding any and all
of the unaccompanied children that had ended up in the
improvised camp. He found his children and they walked
two hundred kilometres to Malemba, in the swamps.

For a year, they lived in a makeshift hut until Makabe's
Mai Mai started running things. 'They were like spirits', he
remembers, 'they wore body parts'. Necklaces made from
hands, ears or lips, and belts made of feet. The Mai Mai
collected pieces of their victims as mementoes and as a
warning to others not to defy them. *Grand-frère* shakes his
head and draws his hand slowly over his face.

When they eventually made it back to Manono, someone else was living in his house and the Rwandans were in
charge. 'They weren't too bad', he says, 'unless you had bad
luck in the evening and they didn't recognize you, then you
might disappear'.

As we leave the port, we pass a modern-looking
speedboat aground among the reeds, by the side of the
road. For a minute I have an image of wild, rich Belgians
water-skiing on the river but then I notice the machine-gun
mount welded to the front of the hull. A gunboat.

Further on, a faded Mobil sign and an exploded
petrol tank rust among the trees. Next to the old petrol
station, quietly asleep under the mango trees, are two boat-
like American cars of the 1950s, decked with swooping tails
and fins. The tyres are flat and their paintwork covered
in dust. They must have been driven here before the road
returned to mud and sand. Now, the few cars that can make
the journey from the port to the town must have four-wheel
drive.

We career through the forest in our overloaded truck, scattering bicycles and pedestrians, trailing four freshly-caught catfish from the back bumper. After fifteen minutes, the road proves too much: a puncture. The children, about fifteen of them, climb down from the towering load and play in the middle of the road, scooping up the sand around them and throwing sticks. Meanwhile, we four adults struggle to change the tyre without a jack. It takes some time; the kids are pleased.

We arrive back at the mission in the afternoon to find a party in full swing. It is the birthday party for the mission choir, reconstituted since the war. The party is in the old schoolrooms of the mission buildings. Illiterate soldiers (some children, no doubt) left testimony of their occupation, a mass of gross and distorted cartoons carved into the walls. Chairs line the walls and the adults sit in a circle, heedless of the recent history written behind them. Young girls in matching uniforms and matching smiles don't seem to notice the artwork as they skip around the room, filling the glasses of the priests and nuns from an old whisky bottle of palm wine – the poison of choice for the clergy when they can't afford beer, which is most of the time.

As I stare at the graffiti of guns, helicopters, aeroplanes and dead bodies, and watch the girls shrieking and playing musical chairs, an unfamiliar feeling grows in my stomach. I suppose this is what drew me here in the first place, to Manono, what I came to this country to seek. It takes me a while to recognize it but here among the children, in the way the nuns gently marshal the girls in their brightly coloured, hand-made clothes, in the deliberate way they serve the palm wine, grasping the bottle with both hands, performing little curtsies, I get a glimpse of hope for Congo.

27

The price of tin

The tailings 'mountain', Manono, circa 1950

MANONO IS A WONDER, a scandal and a tragedy.

Walking through the town, I pass a two-foot-thick steel girder that forms a bridge over an open sewer. A few streets away is an enormous piece of metal, a block of cast iron the size of a small house. This is what I imagine the engine of an oil tanker looks like, except that in the middle of this iron, a mango tree grows. Steel cylinders, several feet thick and ten feet long, litter the roadside. A bulldozer is parked by a house; its tracks rusted together and grass growing though the seat. A bunch of kids waves at me and then returns to swinging on several big round discs spiked with axles and bearing terrifying teeth. It is as though a factory has exploded among the houses but this is not the débris of war.

Much of this equipment was discarded decades ago, some before World War II. Every time the mine was modernized, plant machinery was dumped on the edge of town and, over time, the inhabitants have colonized the wreckage. With wonderful ingenuity, two enormous cones marked 'Nordberg, 40ft Cylinder cone crusher, Milwaukee, WI, USA' have been roofed with grass to make a hut. In every house, metal artefacts salvaged from the mines have become braziers, tables, cooking pots, doorsteps. Recycling has become a way of life. It reminds me of Tatooine, the gangster Jabba the Hutt's planet in *Star Wars*, with its vast robot salvaging yards. Maybe this is what will happen to the Middle East after the oil runs out.

Jean-Baptiste is taking mass this morning so, left to my own devices, I am walking to meet Manono's modern-day aristocracy: the tin buyers.

At the tin-buying station, an old man sits on the floor, a large pile of rock between his legs, his bare feet coated in the white-grey dust of tin ore, like icing sugar. He rakes the pile down with fingers that too are caked in white dust, the nails broken. He steadily picks out rocks that are too white or too crumbly, in which there is insufficient metal. His arms move slowly and heavily; propelling them forward to burrow into the rock is an effort. He looks up mournfully when the manager, Mohammed, comes in with a glass of orange juice for me but then, thinking better of it, looks down and pushes his hands forward to drag the rocks towards him once more.

'Most important is watching the blacks', says Mohammed, indicating the old man who is working no more than six feet from where we sit on a bench. 'They try and steal everything. While they sift here, I must watch.'

Mohammed is a tin trader. He and his cousin, also called Mohammed, are in their early twenties. Born into a Lebanese mining family that trusts no one, apart from its scions, to handle their affairs, Mohammed and Mohammed look after the *Comptoir d'achat cassiterite*, the buying station for tin ore in Manono.

Much has changed in Manono since the ore was first pulled from the ground and smelted in the great machines in the broken warehouses on the western edge of town. Yet so much remains the same. Manono's residents are still shackled to the metal, lorded over by young capitalists from another continent. The industry has reverted to artisanal practice, where everything is done by hand. Light-skinned youths supervise old black men, their fates joined by the global price of tin.

The *comptoir* is a colonial-era building surrounded by a high wall topped with shards of glass. Inside the green gate, beyond its watchman, ancient fruit trees with muscular branches sit in a compound of hard-packed mud. Broad steps go up to a heavy door framed by wide windows. It was once the residence of some important official. The sorting is done in the former drawing room, on a beautiful tiled floor; black and white squares occasionally flash through the piles of grey rock. While the old man claws the dust back and forth, the two Lebanese boys, barely out of school, explain how the tin trade works these days.

Mohammed the first is large, nervous and sweaty; Mohammed the second is slim and composed, with quick black eyes. They are excited and irreverent; I am the first white visitor they have seen for a while, someone they are able to identify with, a friend perhaps.

Today, the hand-mined ore arrives at the *comptoir* in plastic bags. Some is carried on foot from the mine outside the town, some on bicycles from Mitwaba. The boys don't care and they don't ask too many questions. Once the old man and others like him have chosen the good from the bad, the ore is transported to Goma in rickety freight planes flown by Russian pilots. It is a risky business: five planes have blown up in recent months.

'The planes are old and the Russians are greedy. They put seven and a half tonnes when the limit is seven', says Mohammed the second. From Goma, most of the tin avoids the tax man and is smuggled into Rwanda, eventually reaching Belgium then going on to the UK for crushing and smelting.

Manono has not been kind to these hard-working, if prejudiced, boys. The Congolese hate them for making money out of Congo's resources when they cannot; the locals don't have the connections, the capital investment or the means to transport the ore. The boys' time here is short, they hope. Slim Mohammed talks wistfully about moving to London, while large Mohammed dreams of Kinshasa. For now, the high price of commodities makes them prisoners in Manono. If the tin price drops, however, their dreams might come true sooner, and life for the old man will become more complicated.

Tin is a key ingredient in many objects, notably electronic items. For both the old man and the boys, the tin mine is a kind of slavery, not a slavery imposed by man but by a system: across the sea, there is a monster, an insatiable queen bee, that needs feeding and feeding, and for whom no amount of raw material is enough. The strains of feeding the monster inspire greed and terror, pull nations apart, set men against men and press communities into finding it food in the most 'efficient' way possible; that is to say, with the lowest possible cost of labour on which the worker bees can survive. Other parts of the world have laws and media and perhaps unions to restrain the monster from devouring everything. But where there is war, no such framework exists. Some Congolese believe that the fighting is deliberate, that it suits the capitalist thirst for raw materials: without law and order, the monster can exist in its purest form. The supply chain in such a context is raw and untamed and its effects can be cruel.

During the 2006 elections, the church was co-opted to assist with administering the polling, as a neutral party; an awkward situation that was not repeated for the elections of 2011. The bishop appointed Jean-Baptiste to be the returning officer for Manono, another source of jealousy for his colleagues at the mission. At his office in town, the return of the rule of law, of democracy, is tentatively announced on a ragged, rain-soaked scrap of cloth wired to the gate: *Commission electoral indépendante*. But Congo's democracy and governance are, unfortunately, worth about as much as the little piece of orange fabric on which those words are written.

The walls of the election office are pockmarked with bullet scars; in the garden two toddlers play on a swing made from the drive shaft of a truck. Next to the squeaking babies, a production line staffed by young boys sifts and sorts tin. Evidence that, whatever the constitution may say, economics is in fact Congo's highest law.

First, the boys sift the crushed ore in large, battered steel pans made from reclaimed mining equipment. Then they blow on the mix to remove the lighter débris and dust; the heavier tin ore stays at the bottom. The process is familiar to children across Africa, though more often they are choosing rice to eat. Slightly younger boys spread out the remaining dust on rice bags and drag a lump of magnet over the crushed rock: coltan, iron ore and other minerals stick to the magnet; the tin ore remains on the cloth.

'How much do you earn?' I ask.

The boy closest to me smiles and laughs but the others say nothing; they merely keep on at their task. They must know that one kilo of tin currently sells for between five and six dollars; they, I suspect, are not paid more than a dollar a day by the man who runs the shop next to the office.

While I stand there awkwardly trying to engage the boys in conversation, a tall man in a red tracksuit wanders by. He has a short clipped moustache beneath plastic spectacles, a gold chain knocking against his white t-shirt and the air of a man who has something to say. He shifts uneasily from one foot to the other. He is a teacher, he tells me; his name is Gilbert and he is pleased to make my acquaintance.

In this man are vested the hopes for the next generation to escape the trap of minerals, to educate themselves and learn other skills.

Gilbert stands next to me as I watch the boys at their work. The boys put their heads down, necks visibly shrinking, trying to avoid his eyes. I ask if it's usual for neither him nor the boys to be at school; by way of reply he launches into a long complaint about how he could make more money in a week than he does at present, if only he turned to shipping tin instead of teaching. His salary is sixty dollars a month, if it comes at all.

Long ago, he tells me, teachers took matters into their own hands and started charging parents, even at supposedly free government schools. Parents must part with three dollars a year in fees to the government and another four dollars to Gilbert, and every month each child must bring an additional two hundred francs (forty cents), which is divided among the teachers. If the families pay well, and the children come to school often, each teacher can get up to ten thousand francs (fifty dollars) a month.

'Many of the children are digging or choosing tin, so they don't always come to school', he says.

'But how do they get the money to pay you in the first place?'

'Like this', he says, indicating the children crouched in the mud at our feet. 'It's complicated, it is true', he admits with a rueful look.

This is the slippery process by which a blessing can so easily become a curse; a familiar problem. These kids are no different than their peers in many other poor countries in trying to balance the reality of being poor with their hopes for the future. I admire the ambition that lives in the eager movements of the boys, in their arms that shake and draw and pick but their very eagerness is also tremendously sad.

Gilbert walks with me down to the school building, behind the mission. It resembles an art gallery more than a school, with its oddly shaped concrete walls and decorative glass in primary colours. Such a beautiful building, invested with such hope. I am amazed that it has remained intact throughout the war. At the beginning of the twenty-first century, an education seems to be more of a miracle than a right in Congo. In the disaster logic of this place, a bird in the hand is always worth more than two in the bush. If the boys are lured more by the prospect of riches than of learning, sixty years from now they might still be poring over rock, day after day, like the old man in the *comptoir*, and their fingernails will never have a chance to heal.

In the evening, as the rain clouds melt away to reveal pink streaks like entrails scraped across the sky to tell our fortune, Jean-Baptiste takes me to meet Anselm, a man both blessed and cursed by tin. Anselm is slow and heavy on his feet, so we sit on a steel tube discarded from the mine outside his house, a small mud hut set back from the grand boulevard with its useless telegraph poles. He started working for Géomines, the Belgian colonial mining company, in 1958, when he was thirty-six, as an electrician building the power lines at the mine, as well as the pylons in town that are now naked or have been chopped down for scrap, harvested like trees, an insult to his workmanship.

He is angry at the idea that Manono is only defined by the wealth underfoot. The tin boom brought people with skills, livelihoods, to Manono: electricians, doctors, teachers, agronomists, architects, engineers for the railways and the swimming pool. 'We are skilled technicians, we can do other things, not just mining, we want jobs', he says vigorously – as though, despite being over eighty-five, he has plenty of working years left in him. His legs may be reluctant but his mind is still keen and his huge hands work his walking stick like a tool while he talks.

Anselm's view of the past is not rose-tinted; Belgian colonialism was too brutal to allow him the luxury of nostalgia. Géomines paid its workers in food, not money, a practice that the nationalized *Congo Etain* (Congo Tin) continued after independence. When there were strikes, 'they just increased the food, not the money'.

Under the independent secessionist government of Moise Tshombe, those brief years when Katanga was a separate country, it was better. Tshombe paid people well and the hospitals worked. But then the 1970s and 80s saw a long decline, when production shrank year after year and the money slowly dried up until, one day in 1982, *Congo Etain* packed up and left, without telling the workers what was happening, abandoning a mountain of decaying equipment and owing Anselm his final month's wages.

'As you see me, I am officially an employee of *Congo Etain* and they still owe me money!'

Congo Etain is long gone but Anselm knows that its liabilities must have been passed on to the new owners and he intends to give them an earful whenever they show up to reclaim the mine, which, he insists, must happen eventually. He has seen the fortunes of Manono rise and fall in his lifetime, in line with the price of tin, and hopes he can live long enough to see them rise again. He has lived his life in the shadow of the mine and it has left its residue on him. With his walking stick, he digs at the ground. Recently, a delegation, including the minister of mines, came to look at the situation. They called the former employees together and said they will be opening something small and hiring some people.

'One day, they will come back to open the mine again, and then they will call us.'

28

Electric dreams

The flooded engine room of the Manono hydro-electricity plant

MY HEAD HURTS AGAIN. Last night, Jean-Baptiste took me drinking at another place; Chez Gabi, a concrete room with a bucket of dirty water for washing the glasses. Gabi himself mostly slept, while Abbé Jean and his friend, Thierry, argued politics and ignored my struggles to stay awake through the fog of Simba.

Thierry contended that although Manono is a Luba town and he is not a Luba, he could get elected here. He is, he proclaimed, a nationalist, a Congoman and he claimed that Congolese are not ethnically based. More insistent the more he drank, at one point in the session Thierry woke Gabi from his slumber to bolster his thesis.

'If I ran for office would you vote for me?' he demanded.

Gabi's reply was wide-eyed and parochial. 'Of course, I know you well, you come here a lot', as if that were qualification enough.

'You see?' shouted Thierry, undeterred, not comprehending that Gabi had actually undermined his argument.

My headache is not helped by the endless rain. It pours down in great, long, clattering ropes that drag slowly across the wrecked city while the inhabitants huddle in doorways and stare sullenly out at the wall of grey. I am a prisoner of the mission, condemned to fill up my notebook on a tiny desk beneath a calendar sponsored by 'Super Attack' insecticide and a steel-barred window. The window faces on to the courtyard through which I watch the damp priests hop through the mud to their masses, hitching up flowing purple robes with one hand while the other grips an umbrella. They remind me of wounded birds. 'Travel is only waiting', I slowly write in my notebook.

Today I am waiting for the rain to clear so that Jean-Baptiste can take me on the promised tour of the mine.

Jean-Baptiste's job as returning officer for Manono left him custodian of a car and two motorbikes.

'There were no instructions on what to do with them afterwards', he says apologetically, aware that it is a sore point with the other priests.

Mostly, the vehicles gather dust in the mission's garage except when *grand-frère* has goods to collect or someone else pays for the fuel. On condition that I fill up the tank of one of the motorbikes, Jean-Baptiste will show me around, just as soon as the heavens give us a break. Jean-Baptiste understands my journey's purpose and is determined that I see what Manono has become, the havoc wrought by the war and by the vagaries of the price of tin. Jean-Baptiste was born here; his mother still lives in the town she never left. I could not have found a prouder advocate of what Manono was and might be again.

After lunch, the drone of the rain on the iron sheet roof slows to a patter and then a drip, leaving the city water-logged and slick. Life resumes; sails of laundry are raised to catch the breeze and people emerge from houses to leap between puddles like cautious frogs. Jean-Baptiste hollers my name from across the courtyard and wheels a squat red Honda motorbike from the large garage that forms one side of the mission courtyard. I jump on and with a kick and a splutter we are off, weaving between the pools of water and bouncing on to the road.

We leave the mission compound and drive across a packed mud square strewn with schoolchildren in blue uniforms. The walls of the cathedral, which looks as though it was transported whole from Belgium, are decorated with graceful arcs of bullet holes and the roof sports car-sized holes. Ten masses a week are still held here, despite the fact that tiles from the roof fall on the congregation during services. Jean-Baptiste thinks it's funny; he's not worried.

'God protects the faithful', he says.

First stop, fuel. An enormous slippery boulevard, wide enough for six cars, leads us towards the centre of town. The road opens out into a circular expanse with a large metal disc at its centre. Made of steel and ringed with teeth; the disc looks as if it could have been dropped here straight from outer space. A roundabout. There are no tyre tracks in the muddy circle, since the roundabout sees little traffic: these days, there are only three private vehicles in Manono. The petrol seller does a lazy trade, mostly supplying the motorbike-owning community but there aren't many of them either.

In the centre of town, another roundabout is three-quarters ringed by the remnants of Manono's modernist moment. The buildings stand but the great grand sweeps of concrete plazas and arcades are now less a triumph over nature than its prey, cowering in the shadow of the bush, about to be consumed. The concrete has not been very effectively whitewashed; beneath, the former identities of the buildings are visible: *pharmakat*, *supermarché*, *boucherie*.

The doors to these buildings, which once stocked modern medicines from Europe, tinned goods from all over the world and Katanga's finest meat and dairy products, are boarded up. Outside, makeshift stalls are crammed with the twenty-first century fare of Congo's commercial districts: mobile phone credit, machetes, little sugary sweets from Dubai, the usual plastic junk from China, and cigarettes, always cigarettes.

Jean-Baptiste stops to talk to an acquaintance and, in search of a drink, I wander towards a large modern sign: CAFÉ. The concrete pavement has sunk into a cracked and vegetated fringe and the café's faded blue awning matches the faded blue furniture whose colour looks as though it has been diluted by every rainy season since 1959. Inside, a man sleeps with his head pillowed on a long hardwood bar. Here and there, hardwood panelling has fallen off the wall but the magnificent high ceiling is intact. There is no one at the plastic tables arranged randomly within the cavernous space. The place has a forlorn air but I can imagine it with a jukebox and a lick of paint, jumping to the latest tunes.

When I ask about drinks, the man stares blankly up from the bar, his arms crossed. He nods his head at an antique American fridge, huge, sitting on a wooden pallet, its plug-less cable curled beside it on the floor like the tattered tail of an alleycat. Electricity must be a long-lost memory. I stare blankly back at him, confused. He saunters over and opens the big steel door to reveal several empty shelves, and one packed with Coca-Cola. This is all they have, stored in the fridge out of habit.

'I guess I'll have a Coke, then.' The man doesn't laugh. He simply stares back at me as though I am an annoyance, pulls out a Coke, and sets it on the bar. War may destroy nations but not Coca-Cola's supply chain.

I hop back on Jean-Baptiste's bike and we turn off the main boulevard into the garden of a beautiful old villa, built before the modernists unrolled their plans on Manono and before the mining company built their gated town. Tall brick gateposts flank a fine wrought-iron gate that opens on to a gravelled drive, on one side of which a Rwandan tank lies rusting on the lawn. The whitewash is peeling off the brick of the villa and the undergrowth has run riot, obscuring most of the porch.

Beneath a delicious jasmine vine, heavy with scent, on a plastic chair sits a man dressed in a red and white striped tracksuit and spanking clean white trainers. He plays with his sunglasses and multiple gold chains, a rapper in the rainforest. His name is Pascale and he is the 'Gadaffi' of Manono; the nickname bestowed on the petrol sellers because of the former Libyan dictator's habit of providing sub-Saharan Africa with cheap fuel in exchange for other favours. On the porch, several of Pascale's beautiful wives ladle fuel from large drums into Coke bottles. When I complain that the petrol is three times more expensive than in Europe, he shrugs his shoulders and gives a twitch of the head.

'Well, it has travelled far.'

From the port at Mombasa, the fuel comes on trucks through Uganda to Bukavu, and then by plane to Manono. The price of fuel is one of the roots of Congo's distorted economy, the reason everything is so much more expensive than in neighbouring Tanzania, Uganda or Zambia. Jean-Baptiste decants the contents of several Coke bottles into the Honda's tank and, topped up, we return past the cathedral, down the eucalyptus avenue and up to the roadblock that still protects the town of the mining company *societé*, the art deco Utopia of Géomines propaganda.

Today the roadblock is manned by two sluggish soldiers in fatigues. There have very probably been two soldiers or two policemen at this roadblock every day since colonial times. Throughout my journey, I have encountered people clinging to talismans of order: uniforms, flags, offices, titles. Icons of a time when things made sense. People still show up to work day after day, without wages, even with nothing to do.

The soldiers watch us approach, a priest and a white man gripping his waist, on a scarlet Honda. One slowly rises to his feet and fingers the strap of his machine gun where it pinches his shoulder. He puts his hand to his head and unhooks a string; the roadblock's pole goes up and we wobble through.

Even though the war and economic collapse have left Manono, and Congo, a wreck, the colonial geography of the city, and the geography of the minds of its post-colonial citizens, remains intact: the separation of rich and poor, the border between the elite and the rest of the population, the respect for authority, however dubiously gained. Coloni-alism was a contradictory system, at times bloody and exploit-ative, and easily appropriated by the Congolese elite who took over from the Belgians. But it was a system built on order, all the same. It still exerts its control over the land and on the people. It is the weight of the colonial experience, that mixture of deference and defiance, that makes the sol-dier's back stiff and yet his salute lazy. The history of colonial police brutality is audible in Jean-Baptiste's hesitant '*Bonjour*'; the demi-tragic ambition of Manono's Utopia-building plan-ners lives on in the curious, ridiculous power of the skinny, makeshift wooden pole that still divides the town in half.

Through the checkpoint, across the divide, the first house we come to is the UN compound. It is a large square villa, set back from the road. Behind a screen of trees is a wide sweeping drive on which are parked several large four-wheel-drives with 'UN' written on their white bodies in blue letters three feet high. A generator housed in a shipping container chugs by the gate; a radio antenna is nailed to the building's sweeping façade. Two soldiers in the smart uniforms and light blue armbands of the UN peacekeepers smoke cigarettes on the porch, underneath a squared-off roof. That is when I recognize it.

It is the villa in the photograph that I found in the library all those months ago; a world ago. The same Lego

roof, sleek upper floor and wide, rectangular-stepped front-
age and verandah; the same sweep of drive and the trees
along the front, although seen in the heavy grey gloom of
the rainy season rather than in the sharp blaze of the afternoon sun it looks much less romantic. The garden is a
graveyard of discarded containers and fuel barrels, overgrown with grass. A prefabricated office sits along one side
of the garden, obscuring the view of the avenue; on top, a
large satellite dish points its greedy face to the sky. But
there is still some gravel mixed in the mud of the drive and
the trees still tower above the house, humbling it.

The mining company's pride and joy is now the base
of the UN peacekeepers. Such an obvious outcome; I am
almost disappointed. But I have, in a sense, found what
I was seeking. One dream of Congo's future was born and
died here. And it is peculiarly inevitable that this should be
the place where a new dream is being born from the crumbling, rusting ruins of what went before.

Opposite is an empty concrete carcass, marked by
eerily familiar blue portholes and strange geometric patterns. The yacht-like villa is uninhabited and the garden
has almost completely returned to jungle. The house next
door, a low flat house with a covered verandah running
its length, has been slightly patched up and the bush
cut back.

'That is where the Bishop lives', explains Jean-
Baptiste.

Manono's elite lives in these houses: the Bishop,
the head of the Mai Mai militia, the army commander, the
senior UN staff and Manono's only foreign NGO, an Irish
charity with the acronym GOAL, inhabit villas once occupied by Géomine's managers and engineers. But only a
few houses have been rescued from the bush; most

are abandoned. On either side of the road, roofless art deco villas squat amid gardens run riot; vines cover the windows and their walls are scarred with the black of fire. The war has washed over this town and retreated like a tsunami; the rain makes the buildings look as though they are all that is left after the flood. The new commanders who have found themselves washed up here have simply stepped into the repaired ruins of the former masters.

The motorbike weaves in and out of puddles on the potholed marram road and the tall hardwoods give way to a thick clamour of mango trees. At the end of the street, the swimming pool is a trough of rotting fruit buzzing with flies, its floor cracked. The attendant's shed has collapsed. The place has the feel of a graveyard. The steel frame of the high board, without the board, resembles a skeleton with hunched shoulders, staring in melancholy at the mess and wondering if the pool will ever see water again, if Manono's momentary splendour will rise again from these ashes, or if it was all simply a castle built on sand, paid for with tin.

'I used to swim here as a boy', says Jean-Baptiste, 'there were certain days the children from the town were allowed to come'.

There's no one here now.

Next to the pool, the school is empty and, underneath the library's imperious stone lintel, the echoing halls and cracked windows oppose the certainty of its French inscription, carved to endure for generations. Broken glass is scattered everywhere. Further on, elephant grass has stormed the tennis courts like a crowd of over-eager fans, but a proud flash of orange clay is yet visible beneath the green. Next door, in the golf club, the steel poles of bar stools without seats point at the concrete roof. The fairway is brown and furrowed; Manono's hungry residents have ploughed the grass and planted the golf course with cassava.

The layout of the town was originally ordered according to *avant-garde* principles of housing, work, recreation and circulation but these noble ideas have been swept away by a simple basic need: survival. The company town is the starkest example of the science fiction story that Congo has fallen into. This is what the world might look like after an horrendous natural disaster or economic collapse, as humankind, having lost the battle to master the Earth and turn it to our own ends, once again finds itself at its mercy, superstitiously reliant on the soil for the slimmest of pickings, eking out a living amid the wreckage of an industrial past. Rather than a throwback, Congo may in fact represent all our futures.

Huge pylons line the road from the company town up to the mine, every second or third missing, the wires trailing with the vines from the surviving steel frames. Above the villas sits the large squared-off mountain that looks as though its tip was sliced off with a giant knife. The motorbike chuckles past row upon row of disintegrating, numbered, company houses made of brick. Although no work has been done at the mine for decades, the houses burst with the families of former labourers, or their descendants, who will inhabit these houses until someone else lays claim to them.

On the road, we pass families trudging out of town and up to the tailings heaps. The man-made mountain is crawling with figures once again, like ants swarming over food. For now, no one controls the spoils and everyone is busy helping themselves to what they can dig up.

At the top of the hill, the marching column of pylons stops. I look out at almost a square mile of mining wasteland. Dirty ponds, heaps of stones, rusting mining equipment and bright white clay are sprinkled around a creamy white lake. Rusting cranes and trolley tracks that once carried tin ore down to the factories have partly collapsed, a terrifying rollercoaster to nowhere.

A mining company whose website claims it has concessions in Manono says that 200,000 tonnes of tin ore remain here to be exploited. But that company isn't here and every day their estimate is reduced a little further. The small clusters of diggers dotted over the landscape, the majority children and young women, are doing their best to find as much of that tin as possible before the multinationals come back.

Jean-Baptiste stops the bike in the shadow of a huge rusting pipe, which used to pump water out of the lake to allow the miners to get at the tin on the bottom. Knee-deep in the creamy water, a family is panning for ore. The father digs the wet, clay-like soil out of the bottom of the lake, the mother breaks it into chunks and the two children on the shore, one no more than eight, separate it in pans and retain the rock. Because most families in Manono 'farm' tin, there are few vegetables in the market, making food scarce and expensive. The extra dollars made from mining are almost cancelled out by the high cost of food.

Leading away from the hill, we follow another line of rusting pylons to a wide dam. Crowning the barrage is a row of large steel boxes, transformers for the hydro-electric power station, with spiky steel wires poking out, cropped, like a Congolese woman's 'satellite' hairstyle. They look proud and powerful but they are useless now, the wires cut by the Rwandans during the 1998 invasion. It is heartbreaking, such senseless destruction of such a hard-won asset.

'The world wants Congo to be weak', says Jean-Baptiste.

Manono's electric dreams are submerged in the flooded power station. Brown, tea-coloured water rushes through the broken sluice gates, birds nest in the broken roof, vines are choking the turbines and water lilies fill the engine room.

29

The news from Manono

The ruins of the post office, where Radio Manono is stationed

IT'S TIME TO GO but I cannot leave. The pretty villa in the garden, the UN compound, has come to haunt me. Every day, Jean-Baptiste kindly drags the motorbike out into the rain and points its nose past the cathedral, through the road-block and towards the Utopian rectangular house that sits amid the incredibly tall trees, echoing with the thump of the diesel generator. We troop dutifully into the pre-fab office in the garden, the office of the flight co-ordinator, to sit on plastic chairs and wait for him to say again what he has been saying every morning for the last week: there are no flights, the clouds are too low, the planes cannot see to land. How ironic to have spurned the planes to get here and now be spurned by them. Manono's damp is becoming my prison.

The wrecked town in the jungle is the complete expression of what has befallen Congo during the twentieth century. A modern European industrial legacy, first rejected then embraced by the Congolese at independence, is now mourned not for its European roots but for what it represented about Congo, what Congo could be, if only in others' eyes. Like falling in love with someone because they love you. Manono is endlessly fascinating but being stuck here is starting to drive me mad.

Three times a day, I skip through the puddles to share in the tangle of resentment that is communal meal time at the mission. Every priest seems to have a story about the alleged indiscretions or corruption of another. The rest of the time, I stare through the steel bars at the rain or try to sleep through the torpor of the humid afternoons, yearning for a break in the clouds. Accustomed to being able to go where I like, when I like, I find being stationary frustrating but for Manono's residents, who can only dream of going as far as their legs might carry them, remote is merely a state of mind.

In the evenings, one of the priests places his radio on a chair in the courtyard and neighbours come to listen. It's a battered old thing but it picks up the BBC Swahili service from Bush House, on the Strand in London, clear as a bell. Men, and some women, sit or stand on the porch and exclaim quietly at the news from Washington, Kabul, Nairobi. The casuarina trees at the edge of the compound whisper gently but all ears are on the bulletin. As I sit here, I wonder how strange it is that the Swahili broadcast should be the sound of home and if, once I leave Manono, I will ever hear of the place again.

As I have come to know across Congo's ravaged east, news of Manono, and of all the little towns in between, doesn't travel far; only as far as the meagre antennae of the local radio stations will reach. And as my welcome demonstrates, visitors rarely come and residents rarely leave.

The sharp curve of the night has opened its fist; the stars wink down through the trees and are reflected in the puddles. Tonight, Jean-Baptiste is taking me to visit Radio Manono. After dinner, we putter out into the clear air and slick streets, stopping outside a tin hut next to the remains of the old post office. The frangipani tree that grows in the middle of the ruin fills the scene with its wonderful scent and a yellowy light pools in the gap beneath the door.

Inside the hut, which used to be the garage for the post van, several children in rags are clutching cassettes; they share a little bench with a soldier holding a scrap of paper. The hut is divided by a red velvet curtain; behind it, like the Wizard of Oz, at a table piled high with cassettes, car batteries, a microphone and several mobile phones, sit two men: the producer, Vidrack, and the presenter.

Vidrack waves me in and motions for me to sit on the bench facing them whilst placing a conspiratorial finger to his lips. The presenter presses pause on the tape player and reads the news. Today this consists of a verbatim report of a meeting at the government offices, mostly a list of who was in attendance, the *directeur* of this and the commander of that. After the news comes a string of messages that listeners have sent in by text. Then there is an exhortation to 'Keep our town clean' and another saying 'Thank you' to the UN peacekeepers. When the presenter finishes, he says 'And now ...'. There is a long pause. Vidrack and I fix eyes on him with increasing panic. He searches frantically among the pile of cassettes on the desk. Finding the one he wants, he puts it in the machine and presses play ... nothing.

'Please excuse us. That song will come later', he says into the microphone, with an embarrassed glance my way. Vidrack rolls his eyes. The presenter grabs another cassette at random, shoves it into the machine and, thank the stars, bolingo music blares.

Vidrack leaves the table and comes to sit by me. He is a tall, vivacious man, a teacher at the school, who came to Manono in search of work in 2005, when the war was first on the wane. Because he had a background in radio in Lubumbashi, he bought two batteries with help from the UN and began broadcasting in French every evening. He has five children, whom he rarely sees.

'I work too much!' he complains.

The idea behind the station is *politique éducatif*, not the *politique* of the politicians but of promoting education, peace, and reconciliation. Vidrack runs things on a voluntary basis.

'Nobody tells us what to broadcast', he says proudly.

One of the raggedy boys comes in while we talk and hands his cassette to the presenter to be played on the radio. While his song is aired, he sits quietly on a bench behind me, studiously playing with his flip-flops. When it is finished, he receives the cassette with two hands, with no change to his serious face, though as he pulls the curtain aside he gives a little skip.

On the other side of the wizard's curtain, Vidrack introduces me to Safi Christine, a tired-looking woman with friendly eyes. She is a news reporter as well as talk show host but earns her living selling maize in the market. She is also a refugee who fled the fighting in the bush to come here four years ago. When I ask why she volunteers at the station, she replies simply, as though it were the most obvious thing in the world, 'Because I want to bring development to our territory'.

Tonight is her talk show. While we are speaking, several women file in through the narrow door and squeeze the boys and the soldier along the bench with a grumpy shake of their behinds. One evening a week, Christine has an all-female Swahili talk show, when women come to the garage and gather around the microphone for a discussion, broadcast live. This week, the topic is how to handle husbands who drink too much. Last week it was about planting vegetables.

Christine says there is a demand for radio in the nearby villages; people want to know what's going on in Manono. They want to hear the advice of her ladies and broadcast messages to their friends.

'But our antenna is too short, it only reaches sixty kilometres', she laments.

The soldier is the last to have his message read: 'Greetings to the esteemed leaders of 96th Battalion, especially Captain Emmanuel and Colonel Gerome'. He gives a sheepish smile and goes on his way. We follow.

Vidrack escorts Jean-Baptiste and me to the door of the garage. The ground is muddy underfoot and although I must watch my steps, I look up. The rain has drained from the sky and stars shimmer across the black vastness of the night. I feel more than ever that we are not alone here. Radio Manono is like a star, albeit a faint one, glinting at the dark edges of our galaxy, possibly only visible from the northern hemisphere with a very powerful telescope but none the less, energetically sending forth its light. I think back to that day in the library when I stared at the map and wondered about this city of the lost future and what had become of it, and realize how simply impossible it would have been to imagine what I have found. The desire to travel is a funny madness yet sometimes it is essential to go and see for oneself. Even then, how little one can learn about another place, how little in fact, I still know; how foreign Congo remains.

Vidrack pumps my hand in a firm grip and wishes me a safe trip home. He himself has no wish to leave, no desire to escape; this is his home and he is happy, he is smiling. He has a mission.

'Yes, yes. The radio is voluntary but one day it could be profitable. Mama Christine is going to be in charge of marketing.'

The next morning the sky is clear and we are blessed with the first flash of blue in days. The red motorbike zooms forth and Jean-Baptiste secures me a lift on a humanitarian flight leaving at noon. A flurry of goodbyes follows at the mission and then a final tour on the bike along the avenue of eucalyptus trees, past the cathedral and out to the airstrip, with its little emblem of a DC-10 cast in concrete on the side of the angular, decrepit terminal. Half of the runway has been planted with cassava, just like the golf course, but enough remains down the centre for the shaky plane to land.

I walk up the plane steps. At the door I stop and turn. Abbé Jean-Baptiste is astride the red Honda, teeth visible in a broad grin, his hand moving back and forth in a modest wave, perhaps in fear of sudden movements that might disturb his fragile head. We depleted Robert's store of Simba considerably last night, until his wife refused to sell us anymore and packed us off to bed. Jean-Baptiste spent most of the evening trying to persuade me to buy a plot of land in Manono, to be part of the city's resurgence.

'Congo is going to be strong again. It will be a very good investment', he said. And I believe him. He is a dear man with a big, hope-filled, joyous heart; my enduring memory will be of him drunkenly steering the motorbike through the moonlit puddles as, waving an umbrella for balance, I hold on for dear life.

The plane bumps down the boggy runway and in an instant we are above the trees, curving away from the white square mountain, the brown reservoir and the fat muddy snake of a river in the distance. We are heading north, to Goma, once more. The higher we climb, the more intensely the green pulses. Manono is but one island in the vast ocean of forest and bush across which I have sailed a short way.

Before this trip, I knew more about how people in Congo were dying than about how they lived. In some small way, the balance has now been reversed. Congo, like other countries in conflict, is not only a war zone, and neither is it beyond redemption. The identity of the nation is kept alive by people going about their daily chores, in spite of the war and its consequences. Hope lies in the resilience and optimism of people like J-B, the journalist in Goma; the committed NGO workers of Baraka; the Banyamulenge of Bibokoboko; Captain Bwalile and the crew of the *Nyota ya Bahari*; the kind people of Wimbi, Yungu, Talama and Kazimiya; Georges and the Batwa; the nuns of Bukavu and Moba; Leya and her fellow teachers from the Zambian camps; and the priests of Mitwaba and Manono. In their faith that life will continue and, moreover, that things can improve, a peaceful future for Congo will be found.

As the plane climbs higher, I am struck that the stories of these generous and courageous people are heard by so few. And yet it is down there, amidst the noisy clatter of the voices below that the next chapters of Congo's many stories are being written. The only limit to our understanding is our own imagination; the unfamiliar corners of the map are easily populated by demons. Clouds cover Lake Kivu to the north, and before the plane plunges into the grey, I smile as I remember the brave antennae of all the small radio stations across Congo's vast expanse, beacons blinking like lighthouses in the mist, sending out their message to those who choose to listen.

Acknowledgements

Uma Ramiah helped make the idea of the journey a reality and saw me on my way; without her it would have been a different voyage altogether.

Many people equipped me with information and advice beforehand: Celeste Robinson, Maria Burnett, Anneke van Woudenberg, Jonny Donovan, Dupont Nterewa, and Renata Dwan.

I did not record the names of everyone who fed, sheltered, or pointed me in the right direction, and those who are missing from this list are not missing from my thoughts: Neela Ghoshal in Bujumbura, Jean-Baptiste Kambale and Aya Shneerson in Goma; Lt. Col. Ibrahim Bihengo, and Shamis in Walikale; the nuns of the Centre de Amani in Bukavu; Alex Becquevort in Uvira; Yannick Bezy, Jean-François Charriot, and Roelant Zwaanswijk in Baraka; the people of Mizimu, Kazimiya, Yungu, and Talama; Joseph Karombwe and the people of Wimbi; the people of Kalala; the port authority of Kabimba; Rodolphe Bled, Pierre De Backer, Romuald Lucas, and Georges Mbuyu Bintu Kunaha in Kalemie; Samantha Brangeon and Dieudonné Kyezi in

Moba; Stephen Darby and Jo Wells in Pweto; Joseph Musonda and Lubinda Lucas in Kala camp, Zambia; Liliane Bitong Ambassa, Julien, and the Catholic Mission in Mitwaba; *Chef* K. K. wa Kyalwe Kabango Nkasa in Mukanga; Abbé Jean Baptiste Mukalay Malongi and the priests of the Mission Sainte Barbe and Thierry-Noel Mageni in Manono.

The process of turning my rough notes into coherent stories greatly benefited from the clear-eyed input of several early readers: Zanna Jeffries, Uma Ramiah, Gia Rae Wynsryg-Ulmer, Rachel Rosen, Donovan McGrath, Stephen Donovan, and Elfie Rawlence.

A big thank you to Louise Hogan for patiently listening to every word and to her, Zanna Jeffries and Anneke van Woudenberg for essential comments on later drafts. Leslie Lefkow and Georgette Gagnon at Human Rights Watch allowed me the time to get it finished.

I would especially like to thank Bill Sanderson for capturing the spirit of the journey in his beautiful map and the following photographers for allowing me to use their work: Jonny Donovan, Susan Schulman, Mark Craemer, Michael Holthuysen, Pierre Richard and Pierre Douhard.

Finally, there would be no book at all without the unstinting belief and commitment of Sophie Lambert at Tibor Jones & Associates and Robin Dennis at Oneworld Publications.

Illustration credits

Further reading, listening, and watching

When I began researching in the library of the School of Oriental and African Studies, I already had some sense of Congo – its place in European culture has a long history. While my experiences on the ground allowed me to see the country afresh, I had many moments of revelation in the library, both before and after my journey.

The history of central Africa prior to the European incursions is perhaps best captured by Jan Vansina in *Kingdoms of the Savanna* (1966). The first modern accounts of the area are from early Portuguese explorers who in the 1400s visited the mouth of the Congo River where it empties into the Atlantic. The later story of European exploration is grippingly told by the protagonists themselves, notably Richard Francis Burton in *The Lake Regions of Central Equatorial Africa* (1859), written for the *Journal of the Royal Geographical Society* and available online, and by Henry Morton Stanley in his two-volume opus *Through the Dark Continent* (1878). Alan Moorehead's *The White Nile* (1960) paints a compelling picture of the feverish exploration underway between 1856 and 1900. The Swahili side of affairs is lucidly explained in Abdul Sherriff's *Slaves,*

Spices and Ivory in Zanzibar: Integration of an East African Commercial Empire into the World Economy 1770–1873 (1987).

There is a long tradition of hapless Europeans following in the footsteps of the early explorers, a tradition that continues to this day. Among the most amusing are Captain Guy Burrows' *In the Land of the Pygmies* (1898), which provides a startling level of anthropological detail, and the similarly titled film by Aurelio Rossis, *In the Land of Giants and Pygmies* (1925), available online; Rossis's film is an amazing document of the time. A less outmoded book, *The Forest People* (1961), by Colin Turnbull is a firsthand account of his year spent living among the Batwa people.

What King Leopold of Belgium did with the territory Stanley acquired for him is chronicled in Adam Hochschild's classic tale of slavery and colonial exploitation: *King Leopold's Ghost: A Story of Greed, Terror and Heroism in Congo* (1998). The story from there is best presented by Georges Nzongala-Ntalaja in *The Congo from Leopold to Kabila: A People's History* (2002). A haunting relic of Belgian rule is the *Missa Luba* (1958), a recording of the Latin mass based on traditional Congolese songs arranged by a Belgian monk and performed by 'Les Troubadours du Roi Badoin', a children's choir.

There are many books about the assassination of Patrice Lumumba but, in my view, the best summary of all the available information is the rigorously researched film *Lumumba* (2000), directed by Raoul Peck. For a vivid fictional rendering of life after independence, there is, of course, V. S. Naipaul's, *A Bend in the River* (1979). And for a penetrating and witty insight into life in the dog days of Mobutu's rule, read Michela Wrong's definitive account, *In the Footsteps of Mr Kurtz: Living on the Brink of Disaster in Congo* (2000).

The history of Congo's recent wars is still being written, even as the fighting refuses to end. The tale of how the upheaval in Rwanda is still reverberating across the region is described in magisterial detail by Gérard Prunier in *From Genocide to Continental War: The 'Congolese' Conflict and the Crisis of Contemporary Africa* (2009), as well as in more accessible form in Jason Stearns' *Dancing in the Glory of Monsters: The Collapse of Congo and the Great War of Africa* (2011). To learn more about the role of mineral resources in the war, see the Human Rights Watch report, *The Curse of Gold* (2003) and the Global Witness investigation into Bisiye mine, *Faced with a Gun, What Can You Do?* (2009).

Finally, for a beautiful and tragic elegy about the country and the river, I would recommend *Congo River* (2005), directed by Thierry Michel.

Index

Page numbers in *italics* refer to illustrations

About the author

BEN RAWLENCE is Senior Researcher on Africa for Human Rights Watch. His writing has appeared in *The Guardian*, the *London Review of Books*, *Prospect* and the Huffington Post, and he has been a contributor to BBC Radio 4's *From Our Own Correspondent*. He now lives in London.